CHARLES F. STANLEY BIBLE STUDY SERIES

ADVANCING THROUGH ADVERSITY

REDISCOVER GOD'S FAITHFULNESS THROUGH DIFFICULT TIMES

CHARLES F. STANLEY

THOMAS NELSON
Since 1798

Advancing Through Adversity
Charles F. Stanley Bible Study Series

Published in Nashville, Tennessee, by Thomas Nelson. Thomas Nelson is a registered trademark of HarperCollins Christian Publishing, Inc.

All Scripture quotations are taken from the New King James Version.® Copyright © 1982 by Thomas Nelson. Used by permission. All rights reserved worldwide.

Thomas Nelson titles may be purchased in bulk for educational, business, fundraising, or sales promotional use. For information, e-mail SpecialMarkets@ThomasNelson.com.

HB 06.18.2024

First Printing August 2019 / Printed in the United States of America

CONTENTS

ADOPTING A NEW PERSPECTIVE ON ADVERSITY

Bookstores are lined with self-help books. This book, however, is better labeled a "Bible-help" book. When adversity strikes in your life, you will eventually reach the end of your ability to help yourself. Your end point is often God's beginning point. The help that God offers you in His Word—the Bible—is eternal, but it is also timely.

My hope is that, as you engage in this study, you will find yourself referring to your Bible again and again. The Bible is God's foremost communication tool. It is the wellspring of eternal wisdom. It is the reference to which you must return continually to compare what *is* happening in your life with what *should* be happening in you and what *can* happen to you.

So, as you engage in this study, I encourage you to mark specific words, underline phrases, and make notes in the margin of your Bible as you find passages that resonate with you. Although space has been provided in this book for you to record your answers to each of the questions, it may also be beneficial for you to record the insights God gives you in your Bible, which you will be reading regularly long after you have completed this study.

You can use this book alone or with several other people in a small-group study. At various times, you will be asked to relate to the material in one of the following four ways.

First, what new insights have you gained? Make notes about these insights as God reveals them to you, recording them in your Bible or in a separate journal. As you reflect on these new understandings, you are more likely to see how God has moved in your life.

Second, how do you relate to the material? You approach the Bible from your own unique background . . . your own particular set of understandings about the world that you bring with you when you open God's Word. For this reason, it is important to consider how your experiences are shaping your understanding and allow yourself to be open to the truth that God reveals—even if it isn't necessary what you expect. As you do this, you allow God's Word to be a lamp to your feet and a light to your path (see Psalm 119:105).

Third, how do you feel about the material presented? While you should not depend solely on your emotions as a gauge for your faith, it is important for you to be aware of your feelings as you study a passage of Scripture and have the freedom to express your emotions to God. Sometimes, the Holy Spirit will use your emotions to compel you to look at your life in a different or challenging way.

Fourth, in what way do you feel challenged to respond? God's Word may inspire you or challenge you to take a particular action. Take this challenge seriously and find ways to move into it. If God reveals a particular need He wants *you* to address, take that as His "marching orders." God will empower you to *do* something with the challenge He has just given you.

Start and conclude your Bible study sessions in prayer. Ask God to give you spiritual eyes to see and spiritual ears to hear. As you conclude your study, ask the Lord to seal what you have learned so that you will never forget it. Ask Him to help you grow into the fullness of the nature and character of Christ Jesus. Again, I caution you to keep the Bible at the center of your study. A genuine Bible study stays focused on God's Word and will promote a growing faith and a closer walk with the Holy Spirit.

GOD HAS A PURPOSE FOR EVERYTHING

IN THIS LESSON

Learning: Why does adversity come into my life?

Growing: What am I supposed to get out of it?

Adversity has a positive side. I realize this isn't a statement you are likely to hear very often. Your response may be, "Oh, really? You don't know what I'm going through!" But seeing the positive side of adversity is not wishful thinking, denial of reality, or pie-in-the-sky optimism. Rather, it is a statement of faith. The positive side of adversity is rooted in two strong beliefs.

First, *God has a plan and a purpose for the life of every person—including you.* If you want God's plan and purpose to be accomplished in your life, the Lord will go to whatever lengths are necessary to accomplish it. He will not go against your will, but if *your* will is to do *His* will, then He will move heaven and earth to see His will is done in your life. This means God can use adversity to accomplish His plan, further your purposes on the earth, or work His purposes within your life.

Second, *God can turn things to the good for you regardless of the situation you are facing today.* You may think that your life has derailed and crashed beyond any repair. But Scripture says, "We know that all things work together for good to those who love God, to those who are the called according to His purpose" (Romans 8:28).

The Lord has a way of arranging things so good comes from bad. That's His very nature as Redeemer—to take what enslaves us and to use it to free us. When the Lord redeems a situation, He also sends a message to other people who observe what God is doing in our lives. That message may bring about many different reactions—from conviction to repentance to praise. What God does for good in our lives is never limited to us. It is always for others as well.

1. "We are His workmanship, created in Christ Jesus for good works, which God prepared beforehand that we should walk in them" (Ephesians 2:10). What does it mean that you are God's "workmanship"? What does this say about the plans He has for you?

2. How do you tend to perceive adversity? When have you seen something good come out of a time of adversity in your life?

ADVERSITY HAPPENS IN EVERY LIFE

Trials are a fact of life in this fallen world—for both the non-believer *and* the believer in Christ. Jesus said that God the Father "makes His sun rise on the evil and on the good, and sends rain on the just and on the unjust" (Matthew 5:45). He also told those who wanted to follow Him exactly what they could expect from such a life: "Whoever desires to come after Me, let him deny himself, and take up his cross, and follow Me" (Mark 8:34).

This was Jesus' way of warning the people—and us—that if we lead a godly life, walk in His ways, and follow His will, there will be times we are going to have to deny everything that is within us—our desires, wants, goals, and plans—in order to do what He wants us to do. There will be times when we will have to face adversity for our beliefs. He wanted each of us to know that following after Him was not an easy path to take.

Jesus even said, "If anyone comes to Me and does not hate his father and mother, wife and children, brothers and sisters, yes, and his own life also, he cannot be My disciple" (Luke 14:26). Now, what did Jesus mean by this statement? He certainly did not mean that we are to be angry, resentful, hostile, and literally hate our families. Rather, Jesus meant that for us to be obedient to God, there will be times when those we love the most will not understand when we say, "I know this is the will of God for my life—and I must walk in it."

I've known students who have come to me and said, "The Lord has called me to preach. I've told my parents, and they are very upset with me. They don't want me to preach. They are spending all this money on getting me an education to be an engineer, administrator, or whatever, and now I'm saying to them, 'God wants me to preach the gospel.' What shall I do?" My answer is always the same: "You must be willing to be obedient to God, even if you are misunderstood, and trust God to take care of you no matter what comes your way."

Jesus went even further in His warnings about the adversity His followers will face in the Sermon on the Mount: "Blessed are you when they *revile* and *persecute* you, and say all kinds of evil against you falsely for My sake. Rejoice and be exceedingly glad, for great is your reward in heaven, for so they persecuted the prophets who were before you" (Matthew 5:11–12). Many people believe that when you become a Christian, things just sort of clear up. But Jesus' words reveal that some things clear up while some things cloud up. What matters the most is how we choose to respond to the adversity that we will inevitably face in life.

In particular, we have to ask ourselves whether we are going to make it our habit to just walk away when things don't suit us or whether we are going to let God help us to *advance* through the adversity and benefit as a result. Jesus has promised us the best life possible. He has said to us, "I have come that they may have life, and that they may have it more abundantly" (John 10:10). But He never said that life would always be peaceful or full of contentment. Sometimes, He uses the adversity in our lives to point others to His redemptive work.

3. "Beloved, do not think it strange concerning the fiery trial which is to try you, as though some strange thing happened to you; but rejoice to the extent that you partake of Christ's sufferings, that when His glory is revealed, you may also be glad with exceeding joy" (1 Peter 4:12–13). Why should you expect trials to come into your life—even if you are a follower of Christ?

4. What does it mean to "partake of Christ's sufferings"? Why would that be a cause for rejoicing?

5. When is a time that you had to face adversity to pursue what you felt God was calling you to do? What helped you to persevere and follow God's purpose for your life?

A New Perspective on Adversity

In the Gospel of John, we read how Jesus taught this lesson to His disciples by healing a blind man. "Now as Jesus passed by, He saw a man who was blind from birth. And His disciples asked Him, saying, 'Rabbi, who sinned, this man or his parents, that he was born blind?'" (John 9:1–2). The disciples had been taught all their lives that illness was a sign of God's judgment. They had no doubt that somebody had sinned to cause the condition of blindness.

Jesus replied, "Neither this man nor his parents sinned, but that the works of God should be revealed in him" (verse 3). There was purpose to the man's adversity. The disciples saw his blindness as *being caused* by something bad. Jesus taught that the man's blindness was *for the cause of* something good.

Note that Jesus didn't say, "This man is blind because he sinned, but God is going to use it anyway." That would be a much easier statement for us to swallow. Rather, Jesus said that God had a purpose higher than anything the disciples had considered. God intended to use the miracle to bring about something positive and eternal in the man's life and in the lives of those who witnessed his healing.

That puts a new light on any type of adversity we may experience. There is good reason to be concerned about what causes adversity—which we will deal with later—but our greater concern must always be with what results from adversity. Do we allow adversity to throw us back, defeat us, or pull us down? Or do we see adversity as something that can make us stronger, better, and more whole?

Do we regard adversity as a destroyer, or do we see it as carrying the seeds that can produce something beneficial and helpful? Do we see adversity as linked to death, or do we see it as linked to growth and eventually to eternal life? Do we expect the results of adversity to be negative, or do we expect them to be part of God's miracle-working plan?

This book is concerned with how we can *advance* through adversity. Adversity can be a teacher. We can learn valuable lessons from adversity that prepare us to be the people God created us to be—especially as we work through adversity by our faith and according to God's Word. Yes, God has a plan and a purpose for our lives. And yes, God can use whatever comes against our lives for our good.

6. "My brethren, count it all joy when you fall into various trials, knowing that the testing of your faith produces patience. But let patience have its perfect work, that you may be perfect and complete, lacking nothing" (James 1:2–3). What perspective about your trials does James advise you to take in this passage?

....

....

....

....

....

7. James says the "testing of your faith" produces *patience* or *perseverance* in your life. Why is this an important trait for you to possess as a believer in Christ?

8. How have you seen your specific trials lead to greater perseverance in your faith?

GOD HAS A PLAN AND PURPOSE

Every follower of Christ can know that God has a plan and a purpose for their lives. He is continually preparing us to live forever with Him. He has a plan and a purpose for everything that affects us. His love for us is greater than anything we can ask or imagine. He has an infinite number of ways to bring us to new levels of maturity in Christ. He knows who and what to bring into our lives at any given moment in order to accomplish His very specific goals.

But the reality is that in many cases, the only way that some of us will submit ourselves to God's plan is by first experiencing anguish, pressure, trials, or heartaches. For this reason, the Lord will often use adversity to lead us to turn to Him, to trust Him more, to be healed in areas where we need healing, and to grow in ways that we need to grow.

God whispers in our pleasure.
God speaks in our conscience.
God shouts in our pain.
And He really gets our attention when the pain is intense and
beyond our control.

I have seen the reality of this saying in my life and in the lives of countless people. We simply cannot know *every* detail of God's full plan for our lives. From time to time we may receive glimpses of what He still has in store for us, but we are finite—and God is infinite. He alone can see the full scope of our lives and how we fit into His plan for the ages.

God is omnipotent (all-powerful), omniscient (all-knowing), omnipresent (ever-present and eternal), and totally loving. We can trust Him to know how each experience, circumstance, and relationship fits into His plan. We may not see any purpose for some of the troubles that come our way, but God always sees purpose in everything—an *eternal* purpose.

Given this, your first response when adversity comes must be to trust God to make a way through it, to trust God to have a "perfecting good" for you as a result of the adversity, and to trust God there is an eternal purpose for it. God has a purpose for *everything.*

9. "For My thoughts are not your thoughts, nor are your ways My ways.... As the heavens are higher than the earth, so are My ways higher than your ways, and My thoughts than your thoughts" (Isaiah 55:8–9). How high above the earth is the nearest star? What does this teach you about God's plans for your life?

....

....

....

....

....

10. In what areas have you struggled with the idea of adversity or suffering? How do you feel about the prospect that God may have a purpose for adversity in your life?

TODAY AND TOMORROW

Today: God actually uses adversity to bring good things into my life.

Tomorrow: I will ask the Lord this week to change my way of looking at hardships.

CLOSING PRAYER

Father, we want to grow in You and become spiritually mature as believers in Christ. We want to learn the principles by which we are to live this life victoriously—triumphantly, excitedly, happily, joyously—and we know that as we open Your Word, this is what happens. We want to get Your viewpoint so that everything in our lives takes on the sense of delight and transforming joy. For this we thank You and praise You today, in Jesus' name. Amen.

NOTES AND PRAYER REQUESTS

Use this space to write any key points, questions, or prayer requests from this week's study.

THE QUESTIONS WE ASK IN ADVERSITY

IN THIS LESSON

Learning: Why does adversity happen?

Growing: How should I respond?

When adversity strikes, we tend to ask two questions almost as an automatic response: (1) *Why did this happen?* (2) *Who is responsible for this?* Whether we ask them out loud or silently, these questions spring to our minds. The focus of this lesson asks yet another question: "Are these good questions to ask?"

WHY DID THIS HAPPEN?

In many cases, there are good reasons to ask *why* in our world today. *Why* is one of the most potent questions that any person can ever ask.

It is the question at the root of curiosity and discovery. However, when we ask *why* in the face of adversity, our question is nearly always couched in highly personal terms: "Why did this happen to *me*?"

Perhaps the better question to ask is, "Why *not* me?" We live in a fallen world where sin abounds. The human heart has evil intent. Accidents occur. The devil is real, and the Scriptures tell us that he is continually walking about "like a roaring lion, seeking whom he may devour" (1 Peter 5:8). The Lord never promised to keep any of His children from adversity. "He makes His sun rise on the evil and on the good, and sends rain on the just and on the unjust" (Matthew 5:45). Problems, needs, and troubles plague all of humankind, and no one is immune to them.

However, while we cannot assume the Lord will keep us free of all harm, we can count on Him being with us in times of adversity, calamity, tragedy, hardship, and pain. In Psalm 23:4 we read, "Yea, though I walk through the valley of the shadow of death, I will fear no evil; *for You are with me*; Your rod and Your staff, they comfort me."

The better "why" question to ask is, "Why *this*?" Why did *this* happen as opposed to other things? There is an explanation for most things that happen to us. A person may lose a house in a mud slide and face the fact he bought a home in an area prone to mud slides. Or a person may have a serious illness and learn she should have made different choices years before. At other times, the adversity may be outside a person's control, and an explanation can bring closure to a situation. A person may experience a loss from a hurricane, flood, or tornado, and the explanation may be that he lives in a place where hurricanes, floods, or tornadoes are likely to occur. A person may suffer a financial loss on the stock market, and the explanation is that stock market investments have risks associated with them.

Getting to the foundational reason or the logical explanation for adversity can provide valuable information about what not to do in the future. If there is a spiritual root to the adversity, the Lord wants us to face our sinfulness, repent of it, learn from our experience, and have that root of evil pulled out of our lives. Yes, we can learn from adversity and, in so doing, refuse to put ourselves into a position to repeat it.

We should ask, "Why this?" until we get the clearest answer possible. We must also recognize that some problems and difficulties have no answer right now. They may have an answer someday, especially as our understanding of God's purposes increases, but the cause or cure for a particular disease may elude us today. The best recourse is this: trust God for an answer that will bring you peace. That is what you should pursue above all in asking the "why" questions related to adversity. Ask the Lord to give you an explanation to the best of your ability to understand it, and then ask Him to give you the faith to trust His love and to rely on His ability to undergird your life so that you have peace about what you do not know.

1. When have you asked, "Why *me*?" Did you ever get a satisfactory answer? Explain.

....

....

....

....

....

....

2. As you think about that experience, what is your answer to the question, "Why this?"

....

....

....

....

....

....

....

3. When have you seen adversity that was caused by sin? When have you seen adversity that was *not* caused by sin?

WHO IS RESPONSIBLE FOR THIS?

The second question we tend to ask when adversity strikes is, "Who is responsible for this?" Our automatic tendency is to seek someone to blame for our trouble. There are certainly times when others are at fault for the troubles we experience. But not all adversity is caused by, or is even related to, specific individuals. Furthermore, most troubles are multifaceted—they nearly always involve more than one other person or one cause.

It's convenient, of course, for us to choose targets to blame for our adversity. Pointing a finger at another person is a form of denial about any involvement we might have in creating the problem. We must recognize that adversity often comes as a result of our own doing. That's a hard fact to face, but we must do so if we are ever to mature in the Christian life.

Jesus' disciples were not completely off base in their concern about sin being the cause of a man's blindness (see John 9:2–3). Sin sometimes *is* at the root of adversity. Sin sometimes causes a problem. Not all problems are directly caused by an individual person's sin, but all sin ultimately results in some form of death. Sometimes it is physical death, but usually it is a more subtle form of dying. Sin can cause relationships to die, holiness to die, and businesses to die. Certain sins kill ambition and discipline. All of these forms of death result in adversity to some degree. Sin always results in adversity. The old saying, "be sure your sin will find you out," is a truth directly from God's Word (Numbers 32:23). Sin eventually erupts into adversity—it is inevitable.

The classic biblical example of the consequences of sin is the story of Adam and Eve. Their lives were free of adversity at the outset of their creation. They experienced no sickness, death, or suffering of any kind in the Garden of Eden. There was no tension in their relationship with each other. There was no conflict between them and their environment. They lived in a paradise and in complete harmony with God, each other, and nature.

Then things changed because they *sinned*. They disobeyed God by eating of the fruit He had forbidden them to eat. Adam knew what God had said. He knew he was disobeying, yet he willfully chose to disobey. The consequence was beyond comprehension. From the moment Adam sinned, life became full of adversity: Eve experienced pain in childbirth, man and woman had the potential for conflict in their relationship, and Adam struggled against his environment. And to top it all off, both faced living the rest of their days under the shadow of death.

But what about specific examples of sin? Here is one example. A baby is sold into slavery. Why? Because the parents need money. Why? Because they and their older children are hungry. Why? Because there has been a famine in the land. Why? Because there has been no rain and the crops have died. Why? Because the farmers haven't been taught farming skills. Why? Because those who have farming skills haven't shared them. Why? Because people are too busy pursuing other desires. Why? Because people are motivated by greed, the lust of the eyes, the lust of the flesh, and the pride of life—all of which are self-centered and are aimed only at personal benefit (see 1 John 2:16). Why? Because people are sinful.

How many times in that one train of events does sin rear its head? Certainly the parents sin when they sell their baby. But the sin of many others also is involved. Sin never affects only the person who commits it. It is like a stone thrown into a pond: it has a ripple effect.

The other side of the coin is this: sometimes we are the primary reason for our adversity. We sin deliberately to get what we want. We may act innocently, but regardless we are at the core of our problem. We err when we conclude in our pride, "I had nothing to do with this problem!" The fact is that we likely contributed to the problem in some way, and we might have been the primary cause of it for reasons we haven't yet faced.

We contribute to the "sin state" of the world until we receive God's gift of forgiveness, and we set up chains of events in our lives that may bring about negative consequences long after we accept Jesus Christ as Savior. The decisions we make and the actions we take apart from the Lord set up situations that are adversity-prone. Even after we acknowledge Jesus as Lord of our lives, we are in the process of being transformed from living according to sinful, human tendencies into choosing godly righteousness at every turn.

In sum, we help create adversity by our sinful behavior—directly or indirectly, with immediate or long-range results. We must face that fact. If we deny our role in a problem for which we are responsible, we are living in a state of untruth. Jesus said, "If you abide in My word, you are My disciples indeed. And you shall know the truth, and the truth shall make you free" (John 8:31–32). Only the truth can set us free and bring about healing, restitution, and a sure solution. Truth is also necessary to avoid re-creating the problem in the future.

So don't deny your part in adversity. Face up to it and ask the Lord to forgive you for your sin. That's the only way that you can advance through this problem and grow in your relationship with the Lord.

4. "Do not be deceived, God is not mocked; for whatever a man sows, that he will also reap. For he who sows to his flesh will of the flesh reap corruption, but he who sows to the Spirit will of the Spirit reap everlasting life" (Galatians 6:7–8). How are

you mocking God when you try to deny your own responsibility for adversity?

5. What does it mean to "sow to the flesh"? Give examples.

6. What does it mean to "sow to the Spirit"? Give examples.

BLAMING ADVERSITY ON SATAN

A number of years ago, the expression "the devil made me do it" was quite popular. That wasn't a new idea, of course. Eve tried that excuse in the Garden of Eden!

Blaming the devil for adversity is a convenient means of self-justification. Many people like to make the devil their scapegoat. They refuse to be responsible for anything bad that comes their way. But again, that's living in untruth. The devil probably doesn't deserve as much credit as we give him.

I am not denying the power of Satan. The devil is real, alive, and active in our world. He is one-hundred percent evil, and everything he does is intended to destroy God's children (see John 10:10). But

I *am* saying that we err if we blame Satan to the point that we deny our sin or deny that someone other than Satan may have been a factor in our adversity. Satan is the father of all lies and the instigator of all temptation, but he is not the father of all adversity. We do a good job of bringing about adversity all on our own, even without direct help from Satan.

There are times when people open themselves up to evil and as a result experience oppression by demons. More often, influence of demons generally intensifies as willful, sinful behavior progresses over time. In the vast majority of cases, the devil does not make us commit sinful behavior. The devil tempts, and we do the sinning!

At other times, Satan is a direct source of adversity. He is clearly called our "adversary" in the Scriptures—a name directly linked to adversity. The clearest example in the Bible is the story of Job. His friends and family tried to link his adversity to his sin or lack of faith. The Bible says, however, that Job was "blameless and upright, and one who feared God and shunned evil" (Job 1:1). From God's perspective, Job was a model of human righteousness.

Satan, however, argued that Job was righteous only because God had blessed him in many wonderful ways. So the Lord said, "Behold, all that he has is in your power; only do not lay a hand on his person" (verse 12). Satan then set out to destroy all that Job had, but Job continued to serve God and walk in His ways.

So Satan made another request: "Skin for skin! Yes, all that a man has he will give for his life. But stretch out Your hand now, and touch his bone and his flesh, and he will surely curse You to Your face!" And the Lord said to Satan, "Behold, he is in your hand, but spare his life" (2:4–6). Satan then struck Job with painful boils. Note that God gave permission for Satan to strike Job, but the striking itself and the motivation for the adversity came from Satan.

Satan is the ultimate enemy of our souls. Spiritual torment comes from him. In many ways, this form of adversity is the most painful—those who experience it usually are filled with fear, plagued with doubts, and never at peace. The solution for this type of adversity is to turn to God and trust Him with every aspect of our lives.

In the end, we must come to the conclusion that regardless of *who* is responsible for our adversity, only one Person can help us out of it: the Lord Jesus Christ. He is our sure help in times of trouble (see Psalm 46:1). We also must recognize an answer to the "who is responsible?" question may elude us. We may never know who is responsible, from God's perspective, for the trouble in which we find ourselves. But we can know the source of our solution, our healing, our deliverance, our redemption, our salvation. His name is Jesus.

7. "But each one is tempted when he is drawn away by his own desires and enticed. Then, when desire has conceived, it gives birth to sin; and sin, when it is full-grown, brings forth death" (James 1:14–15). What does it mean to be "drawn away" and "enticed" by your own desires? Give specific examples.

8. How is desire "conceived"? How does it give birth to sin?

HOW SHOULD WE
RESPOND TO ADVERSITY?

The questions "Why did this happen?" and "Who is responsible?" cause us to look away from our adversity and into our lives and past events. But asking, "How should I respond to this adversity?" turns our focus forward. It is the most productive, helpful, and positive response we can make in a time of trouble.

The disciples of Jesus no doubt stood at Calvary wondering why such a horrible thing as the crucifixion of their Master had taken place. Their dreams were shattered. They had seen their beloved leader suffer and die before their very eyes. They might well have asked, "Who was responsible for this?" The Roman or Jewish leaders? The clamoring crowd that had been so easily assembled and whipped into a frenzy? Sin? Satan? God? The answer is *yes* to all!

Christ's response was to allow God to use a terrible form of adversity to fulfill His plan of salvation and to achieve an eternal and marvelous good. That is the same response you are to have today. When adversity strikes, you are to boldly face the situation and your future and ask, "What now?" You must avoid the tendency to get bogged down in the endless pursuit of who is responsible for this trouble and turn your focus to a much more positive, forward-looking question: "Who can bring me *out* of this trouble?"

The only way you can advance in your spiritual life in times of adversity is to look up to Jesus and forward into your future with Him. He is the answer to the *why* and *who* questions!

9. "[Jesus] withdrew about a stone's throw beyond them, knelt down and prayed, 'Father, if you are willing, take this cup from me; yet not my will, but yours be done'" (Luke 22:41–42). How did Jesus respond to the adversity He was facing?

10. What does Jesus' example teach you about responding to adversity? How are you looking to God to bring you through this time of trouble in your life?

....

....

....

....

....

TODAY AND TOMORROW

Today: The most important response to adversity
is to ask God, "How should I respond?"

Tomorrow: I will ask the Lord to show me what
He wants me to learn through times of testing.

CLOSING PRAYER

Father, You love us in ways we wouldn't interpret as love, because we don't see things the way You do. We thank You for every adversity You allow in our lives. Today, we pray the Holy Spirit of the living God—Your Spirit—would work His wonderful work of grace in the lives of those who are unsaved. We pray they would invite the Lord Jesus Christ as the Great Burden-bearer to share their load and to walk with them through the adversities of life. Amen.

NOTES AND
PRAYER REQUESTS

Use this space to write any key points, questions, or prayer requests from this week's study.

IS ADVERSITY EVER CAUSED BY GOD?

IN THIS LESSON

Learning: Does God cause bad things to happen?

Growing: What are God's purposes when adversity strikes?

Does God ever cause adversity? The comfortable but theologically incorrect answer is *no*. Many people teach that God never sends an ill wind into a person's life, but this position cannot be justified by Scripture. The Bible teaches that God does send adversity—but within certain parameters and always for a reason that relates to our growth and eternal good.

Does this make God any less loving or any less good? No. Neither is a parent who disciplines a child any less loving or good. In fact, the consistent discipline of a child is a hallmark of good parenting.

God's discipline is part of His attribute of flawless goodness. A good and God would do nothing less than lovingly discipline His children for their benefit.

GOD MAY BRING ADVERSITY

Consider the life of the apostle Paul. There can be no doubt the Lord loved him. God called him in a dramatic way to become an apostle to the Gentile world. Paul knew God intimately and followed Him explicitly. But that does not mean that he was spared all adversity.

In 2 Corinthians 11:23–28, Paul listed many of the adversities he faced during the course of his ministry. Some of this adversity was of his own doing. He was a bold man who refused to compromise and ruffled some feathers along the way. But much of the adversity was caused by others—those who refused his ministry and persecuted him with beatings, floggings, imprisonment, and stonings. Paul was also robbed on occasion, and he faced storms, weariness, toil, sleeplessness, cold, hunger, and thirst.

Most people would have given up after facing just a few of these adversities. "Let somebody else take a turn at being an apostle." But not Paul. His great love and concern for the Lord and the churches that he had established drove him forward.

"But," you may say, "I see no mention of adversity caused by God in the list of Paul's struggles." In 2 Corinthians 12:7–10, Paul wrote:

And lest I should be exalted above measure by the abundance of the revelations, a thorn in the flesh was given to me, a messenger of Satan to buffet me, lest I be exalted above measure. Concerning this thing I pleaded with the Lord three times that it might depart from me. And He said to me, "My grace is sufficient for you, for My strength is made perfect in weakness." Therefore most gladly I will rather boast in my infirmities, that the power of Christ may rest upon me.

Therefore I take pleasure in infirmities, in reproaches, in needs, in persecution, in distresses, for Christ's sake. For when I am weak, then I am strong.

We don't know what Paul's "thorn in the flesh" was, because God doesn't tell us. I think there is a good reason why He does not. If we knew the nature of Paul's thorn in the flesh, any person who experienced that same ailment or form of attack would say, "Well, I have the same thing that Paul had." That could be a cause for boasting or a false explanation.

We do know Paul's thorn in the flesh *was given to him* and was *for a purpose.* Paul concluded that a "messenger from Satan" had delivered the gift, but that the giver of the adversity was the Lord Himself. Paul pleaded with God to take back the gift, but the Lord refused, saying, in essence, "I have a purpose for this in your life." Furthermore, God gave Paul the thorn in the flesh for *his ultimate good*: "Lest I should be exalted above measure by the abundance of the revelations." Paul was referring to visions and revelations he received from the Lord, including one in which he was caught up to heaven (see 2 Corinthians 12:1–4). Paul perceived the Lord had given him a thorn in the flesh so he wouldn't be "exalted above measure" and so the Lord would be recognized as the sole cause for successful ministry in his life.

We know that Paul regarded the thorn in the flesh as coming from the Lord because he did not deal with it in the same way he dealt with satanic attack, persecution, or his own sinfulness. When confronted by spiritual attacks, Paul rebuked the enemy soundly and brought deliverance to those who were under Satan's influence. Paul stood up to persecutors, and he had no fear when it came to confronting them or arguing with them. Throughout his letters, he was quick to acknowledge his own past sinful nature. But in this instance, Paul reported a conversation with the Lord. He acknowledged the Lord had a purpose in giving him a thorn in the flesh and that he would submit to the purpose.

Being submissive to God's chastisement isn't easy. The first response is to flee from it or shake it off. It takes a certain amount of spiritual maturity to admit, "God may have a message for me in this adversity. He may be trying to deal with me in some way so I might grow in my faith and become more like Jesus."

1. Why did Paul believe God had given him a "thorn in the flesh"?

....

....

....

2. Paul wrote, "When I am weak, then I am strong" (2 Corinthians 12:10). How would you explain this paradox in your own words?

....

....

....

....

3. When have you seen God's strength made more visible because of your own weakness?

....

....

....

....

God May Give the Permission

In the previous lesson, I referred to how the Lord allowed Satan to test a man named Job by attacking his possessions, his children, and his own health and well-being. The story of Joseph, the son of Jacob, is another lesson on how God grants permission for adversity to enter our lives so an ultimate good might be accomplished.

Joseph was greatly loved by his father—a fact that caused his older brothers to be jealous of him. Joseph shared two dreams with them, in which he was exalted and his brothers bowed to serve him. This was more than the brothers could take. Jacob rebuked Joseph for telling the dreams, yet the brothers were determined to teach him a lesson (see Genesis 37:1–10).

Joseph later traveled out to the place where his brothers were tending their flocks. When they saw him coming, they first conspired to kill him, and then decided to strip him of his tunic and throw him into a pit. They finally sold Joseph to a caravan of Midianite traders. The Midianites then sold him to Potiphar, an officer of Pharaoh (see verses 11–28, 36).

Joseph rose to prominence in Potiphar's house, but Potiphar's wife falsely accused him of trying to seduce her, and he was sent to prison. Joseph rose in leadership among the prisoners and even helped Pharaoh's chief butler out of difficulties. But the chief butler forgot Joseph for two full years before mentioning him to Pharaoh (see Genesis 39–40).

Talk about a long string of adverse situations! Few of us have ever been persecuted by our family members, an employer, and then a peer. Joseph endured adversity year after year. Then, in one day, his destiny was fulfilled. His adversity was reversed. Joseph interpreted a dream for Pharaoh and was put in charge of the nation's harvest—an important and prominent position. He was given Pharaoh's signet ring so he could conduct business in Pharaoh's name. He was given a chariot and a gold chain, which indicated to the entire nation he was second in command. What a day that must have been! It surely must have felt like a dream to him.

Joseph was ultimately able to help his family during a time of severe famine. In the course of saving their lives, his brothers did bow down to him (see Genesis 41–47, 50). Later, after Jacob had died, the brothers feared Joseph would seek vengeance against them for selling him to the Midianites. But Joseph said to them, "Do not be afraid, for am I in the place of God? But as for you, you meant evil against me; but God meant it for good, in order to bring it about as it is this day, to save many people alive" (50:19-20).

Joseph concluded that God had been in charge all the time. Nothing had happened to him that was outside of God's permissive will. Everything he had experienced was part of a divine plan. In fact, some Bible scholars conclude that the "man" who directed Joseph to his brothers at Dothan was an angel of the Lord (see 37:15-17). If so, the man was directing Joseph to the very brothers who would sell him into slavery.

Did God want Joseph to be subjected to such adversity? The Bible doesn't say that directly. But we can conclude that God *permitted* the adverse situations to occur in Joseph's life. The Scriptures tell us that Joseph trusted the Lord continually. The adversity had nothing to do with judgment on Joseph, nor was it a form of chastisement.

Certainly, the Lord could have put a stop to the adversity at numerous points. He could have stopped Joseph from travelling to the place where his brothers were tending their flocks. He could have prevented the brothers from throwing him into the pit. He could have averted the travel plans of the Midianites or allowed Joseph to escape from their hands. He could have provided witnesses to counteract the false claims of Potiphar's wife. He could have caused the chief butler to remember Joseph sooner. Instead, the Lord chose to allow Joseph to endure the hardships.

Finally, the Bible tells us the Lord was *with* Joseph in each experience and blessed Joseph *in spite of* adverse circumstances. That's good news for us! When we look at Joseph's life, we see he moved from strength to even greater strength. Each adverse situation prepared him in some way for the leadership role that he would eventually assume. Joseph didn't bow down to defeat. Rather, those who sought to defeat Joseph bowed down to him.

You can anticipate the same outcome. When you belong to the Lord, any adversity you experience is subject to His power and grace.

He never stops being in charge of your life. He never loses authority over you or the circumstances that affect you. God is always in control. Therefore, you must conclude the Lord allows adversity to enter your life on occasion. He uses adversity to fulfill His purposes in you and in the lives of others. Joseph's destiny wasn't limited to himself or even to his own family. It involved all the tribes of Israel and the destiny of a nation.

4. What were some of the circumstances, coincidences, and people in Joseph's life that conspired against him? When have you experienced anything similar?

5. If you had been in Joseph's place, how might you have responded in any of those circumstances? What was Joseph's response?

GOD WILL LIMIT ADVERSITY

God may allow Satan to persecute us and harass us, but He also puts a limit on the amount of adversity He allows Satan to send our way. In the case of Job, God stopped Satan the first time with the limitation "do not lay a hand on his person" (Job 1:12), and the second time with the limitation "spare his life" (verse 6). Satan had to comply with God's commands, and Satan has to comply today with God's limitations on the amount of adversity you and I experience as God's children. That's good news for us. There is a limit to adversity. It will come to an end.

A woman said to me that one of her favorite phrases in the Bible was "and it came to pass." She said, "Just think, *it came to pass.* It didn't come to stay!" That's a good attitude to have about adversity. Today's troubles are just that—*today's* troubles. A season of trouble is just that—a *season* of trouble. Crises pass, circumstances change, situations improve. God works in and through adversity to bring it to an end according to His timetable.

Daniel noted this in his prophetic word when he said the "beast" would be allowed to persecute the saints "for a time and times and half a time" (Daniel 7:25). The word *persecute* in this passage literally means "wear out." The enemy of our souls attempts to grind us down, wear us out, wring us dry. But God says, "Not completely." There is nothing Satan can do to us beyond God's limits if we continue to trust God and resist the devil.

Furthermore, we have the assurance that God will be with us and that He will strengthen us during times of adversity. As the apostle Paul wrote to one body of believers, "I know how to be abased, and I know how to abound. Everywhere and in all things I have learned both to be full and to be hungry, both to abound and to suffer need. I can do all things through Christ who strengthens me" (Philippians 4:12-13). God will provide the strength we need to get us through the adversity.

6. How do you respond to the idea that God will sometimes *allow* Satan to bring adversity into our lives? Why do you think He allows the enemy to bring such trials?

7. What are some ways the Lord has strengthened you during times of adversity? What did you learn about yourself during those seasons in your life?

GOD'S HELP IS FOR THE BELIEVER

God uses adversity in the life of the believer for many purposes—all of them ultimately good. He limits adversity in the life of the believer. He strengthens the believer to endure the trials the enemy brings. But none of these statements can be made on behalf of the unbeliever. This is because the unbeliever stands before God in an enemy position—a position of estrangement and alienation from the Lord. The unbeliever is loved but is also subject to harsh treatment if he confronts God's children or attempts to interfere with His plans.

Time and again, we read of God showing no mercy to His enemies. He defeats them soundly and decisively. To be an enemy of God is to be in a precarious position. The unsaved person is in a spiritually lost state, and he or she is in danger physically, emotionally, and mentally. The enemy has total access to an unbeliever—an access limited only by the prayers of God's faithful people on behalf of that person.

God responds to the unsaved person's willful sin and acts of transgression. The Lord does not sit on His throne and survey the world and take potshots at people in a willy-nilly, capricious manner. He sets out to show that He is in control. God is not a bully. Rather, the Lord moves against sin. God is just and righteous. He *must* counteract sin.

This was Jeremiah's message in the book of Lamentations when he concluded the Lord does not "afflict willingly" (3:33). The Lord does not want adversity for His people, but He is responsive to our actions. And when we sin, God responds to our sin even as He loves us beyond measure. As Moses wrote, "The LORD is longsuffering and abundant in mercy, forgiving iniquity and transgression; but He by no means clears the guilty" (Numbers 14:18).

As a believer in Christ, your response should be threefold when you confront adversity. First, your response should be, *"Deliver me!"* This was repeatedly the cry of God's people throughout the Scriptures. Second, your response should be, *"Thank You, Lord."* Acknowledge the Lord may be dealing with you to show you something that needs to be changed or something you need to do so you might become more like His Son. Third, your response should be, *"I trust You."* As you yield to what the Lord wants to accomplish in you, rest in faith that God has a plan and is in control—and that His hand on your life is one of unconditional love and omnipotent power over the adversity.

8. "Do you not know that friendship with the world is enmity with God? Whoever therefore wants to be a friend of the world makes himself an enemy of God" (James 4:4). What does it mean to have "friendship with the world"?

9. "Trust in the LORD with all your heart, and lean not on your own understanding; in all your ways acknowledge Him, and He shall direct your paths" (Proverbs 3:5–6). What does it mean to "lean on your own understanding" and acknowledge God "in all your ways"? Give examples of when you have taken each course of action.

10. "For He does not afflict willingly, nor grieve the children of men" (Lamentations 3:33). If God "does not afflict willingly," why do you think He sometimes allows grief in your life?

_____

_____

_____

_____

TODAY AND TOMORROW

Today: God does send adversity into my life, but He does it for my good—not for my suffering.

Tomorrow: I will thank and trust the Lord during trials— even as I ask Him to deliver me.

CLOSING PRAYER

Father, we thank You for sending us difficult times, trials, and tribulations. We think about the fact You are such a loving heavenly Father that You are willing to allow us—as Your children—to go through times of trouble in order to build us up, strengthen us, and mature us in our faith. We thank You, Lord, for the lessons that You are teaching us by allowing adversity to confront us each day. You watch, build, strengthen, establish, and confirm, but You don't take away the hurt until You have accomplished Your purpose. Thank You, Father, for the work that You are continuing to do in each of our lives. Amen.

NOTES AND
PRAYER REQUESTS

. . . .

Use this space to write any key points, questions, or prayer requests from this week's study.

THREE REASONS WHY GOD ALLOWS ADVERSITY

IN THIS LESSON

Learning: What is the purpose of adversity in the first place?

Growing: What am I supposed to be learning from this?

If we are willing to acknowledge that God uses adversity to make us more like Jesus, then we must ask ourselves a question when a crisis hits: *What reasons may the Lord have for this adversity in my life?* Adversity, trials, and heartaches operate as lessons in the school of experience. They bring us new insight and understanding. They alter our perception of the world and God and lead us to change our behavior. The Lord, of course, is the ultimate Teacher. He is the One to whom we must look for the meaning of any lesson related to adversity.

In the Bible, we find that God often allows adversity for three reasons:

- To get our attention.
- To lead us into self-examination.
- To help us change our belief or our behavior.

GOD USES ADVERSITY TO GET OUR ATTENTION

The first goal of a teacher is to get a student's attention. After all, you can't teach a student who isn't listening to you. In the same way, the Lord will sometime use adversity in your life to cause you to pay attention to Him in a new way.

This is what happened to Saul of Tarsus as he traveled on the road to Damascus. It was not a routine bureaucratic trip for Saul—he intended to bring great persecution on the Christians in that city. The Bible tells us that Saul was "breathing threats and murder against the disciples of the Lord" (Acts 9:1). Saul was so much given to his task that he was nearly consumed by his murderous intent.

However, God got Saul's attention as he made his way to the city of Damascus:

As he journeyed he came near Damascus, and suddenly a light shone around him from heaven. Then he fell to the ground, and heard a voice saying to him, "Saul, Saul, why are you persecuting Me?" And he said, "Who are You, Lord?" Then the Lord said, "I am Jesus, whom you are persecuting...." So he, trembling and astonished, said, "Lord, what do You want me to do?" Then the Lord said to him, "Arise and go into the city, and you will be told what you must do." And the men who journeyed with him stood speechless, hearing a voice but seeing no one. Then Saul arose from the ground, and when his eyes were opened he saw no one. But they led him by the hand and brought him into Damascus (Acts 9:3–8).

Saul definitely had a wake-up call from the Lord that day. In one unforeseen moment, God gained his undivided attention, striking him with the adversity of blindness and no doubt humiliating him in front of his traveling companions as he groveled in the dust of the road. But God had Saul exactly where He wanted him.

Saul was more than ready to listen when the Lord asked, "Why are you persecuting Me?" Up to that point, Saul thought he was only persecuting Christians, not the Lord Himself. A period of intense adversity resulted in a complete turnaround, to the point that he was proclaiming Jesus in the synagogues within a matter of days. Those who witnessed this abrupt change were amazed by what they saw:

So when he had received food, he was strengthened. Then Saul spent some days with the disciples at Damascus. Immediately he preached the Christ in the synagogues, that He is the Son of God. Then all who heard were amazed, and said, "Is this not he who destroyed those who called on this name in Jerusalem, and has come here for that purpose, so that he might bring them bound to the chief priests?" (Acts 9:19–21).

When we hear a story such as this one, it is easy to see the value of adversity. If it took temporary blindness and humiliation to get Saul's attention, it was certainly worth it, for through Saul—known to us as Paul the apostle—the gospel was preached and churches were planted across the Roman world.

Perhaps one of the best responses to adversity that strikes you suddenly with a God-intended message is to turn to Psalm 25 and make it your personal prayer:

To You, O LORD, I lift up my soul.
O my God, I trust in You;
Let me not be ashamed;
Let not my enemies triumph over me.
Indeed, let no one who waits on You be ashamed;
Let those be ashamed who deal treacherously
    without cause.
Show me Your ways, O LORD;
Teach me Your paths.
Lead me in Your truth and teach me,
For You are the God of my salvation;
On You I wait all the day.
Remember, O LORD, Your tender mercies and Your
    lovingkindnesses,
for they are from of old.
Do not remember the sins of my youth, nor my
    transgressions;
according to Your mercy remember me,
for Your goodness' sake, O LORD.

Don't delay in responding to the Lord when He makes a move to get your attention. Respond quickly and humbly. Hear what He has to say to you.

1. If you had been in Saul's position, how might you have reacted to being suddenly struck blind?

2. How did God use physical blindness to give Paul sight? How has He used adversity in your life to provide something better than what you lost?

_____

_____

_____

_____

_____

_____

_____

_____

ADVERSITY LEADS US TO SELF-EXAMINATION

As mentioned, at times God will see fit to allow a little adversity into our lives to motivate us to self-examination. The winds of adversity blow off the surface issues and force us to cope with things on a deeper level. Adversity removes the cloak of what we are supposed to be to reveal the truth of who we are. The "real us" shows through.

As believers in Christ, we are to examine ourselves in an ongoing and regular way. Paul encouraged the Corinthians, "Let a man examine himself" (1 Corinthians 11:28). In other words, "Take an inquisitive look inside and discover what is driving you, motivating you, and enticing you."

God does not want negative elements from the past to lie around in our lives and cause us to deteriorate. Each of us is the temple of the Holy Spirit, and He wants us to be clean and usable vessels. There is no reason to allow the rubbish of the past to remain in our lives for years—old memories, haunting temptations, the baggage of unresolved hurts and unreconciled relationships. The Lord wants us to be free of anything that might keep us in bondage—mentally, emotionally, psychologically, or spiritually. When we become complacent and accept the hurts of the past as part of who we are, the Lord may bring a little adversity to lead us to face who we are and pursue instead who we might be in Christ Jesus.

The longer we allow important spiritual issues to go unresolved, the greater their negative potential. The deeper the roots, the greater our resistance and the more painful the excavation process. That is one of the reasons that God keeps the pressure on us. He knows that if He lets up, we will return to our old ways.

3. "Search me, O God, and know my heart; try me, and know my anxieties; and see if there is any wicked way in me" (Psalm 139:23–24). What does the process of God's searching your heart involve? How does He use adversity in that process?

_____

_____

_____

_____

_____

4. "Let us search out and examine our ways, and turn back to the LORD; let us lift our hearts and hands to God in heaven" (Lamentations 3:40-41). How exactly does a person "search out and examine [his] ways"? Give practical examples.

_____

_____

_____

_____

_____

_____

_____

5. What does it mean to "lift our hearts and hands" to God? Give practical examples.

....

....

....

....

....

....

....

....

EFFECTIVE LESSONS LEAD TO CHANGES IN BEHAVIOR

Teachers often prepare behavioral objectives for their classroom lessons. These objectives list clear and measurable behaviors the teacher wants students to show as proof they have learned the lesson. The lessons the Lord teaches through adversity are ultimately for that same purpose: a change in behavior—including a change in the belief that gives rise to behavior. It isn't enough the Lord gets our attention or that we engage in self-examination. We can see a problem and know ourselves thoroughly, but unless we change our response to God in some way, we will never benefit fully from adversity or grow as a result of it.

Self-examination may be a painful experience for you. But remember, whatever you find within yourself, Jesus Himself came to help you carry that burden to the cross and deal with it there once and for all. He has your best interest in mind. He knows that pain sometimes paves the path to complete healing and restoration of the inner person.

If you are willing to allow God to bring the inner rubbish of your life to the surface, and if you are willing to change what needs to be changed in your life, you will emerge from adversity closer to Christ, more mature as a child of God, and with far greater potential to reflect the love of God to the world around you.

6. "Blessed is the man who walks not in the counsel of the ungodly, nor stands in the path of sinners, nor sits in the seat of the scornful; but his delight is in the law of the LORD, and in His law he meditates day and night" (Psalm 1:1–2). Notice the sequence: walk, stand, sit. What does this suggest about the process of sinful habits?

7. How can self-examination lead you to delight "in the law of the LORD" and keep you from walking in the counsel of the ungodly? What role might adversity play in this?

Our Continual Growth Is the Lord's Desire

The Lord has made no provision for any of us to stop at some point in our growth toward being like Christ. We may never fully arrive at His perfection, but we are always to be striving to become more like Him. We must never become complacent about who we are or satisfied that we have developed all the character that is necessary. Character building and spiritual maturity are both lifelong processes. As the author of Hebrews wrote:

> Let us lay aside every weight, and the sin which so easily ensnares us, and let us run with endurance the race that is set before us, looking unto Jesus, the author and finisher of our faith, who for the joy that was set before Him endured the cross, despising the shame, and has sat down at the right hand of the throne of God (Hebrews 12:1–3).

When we become complacent, the Lord may permit adversity to jostle us forward in our spiritual walk. God doesn't merely seek to get the attention of sinners, but He also wants the full attention of those who love Him. God compels all of us to engage in periodic self-examination so we may face up to our own sin and the smudges on the soul that we acquire in the course of our lives. And always, the Lord wants us to do the difficult work of changing our beliefs and our behavior so that what we believe and do are in total harmony with what Jesus would believe and do if He were walking in our shoes today.

So move forward. Keep growing. Never stop looking forward and upward to Christ Jesus.

8. "The night is far spent, the day is at hand. Therefore let us cast off the works of darkness, and let us put on the armor of light. Let us walk properly, as in the day, not in revelry and drunkenness, not in lewdness and lust, not in strife and envy. But put on the Lord Jesus Christ, and make no provision for the flesh, to fulfill its lusts" (Romans 13:12–14). What does it mean to "put on the Lord Jesus Christ"? Give practical examples.

9. What is the "armor of light"? Why does Paul speak of armor in this passage rather than normal clothing?

10. What are some ways you are persevering in the "race" that God has set before you? What spiritual growth can you see as you look back on your life?

TODAY AND TOMORROW

Today: God uses adversity to get my attention and to lead me to examine myself and change.

Tomorrow: I will prayerfully examine my life, asking God what needs to change.

CLOSING PRAYER

Father, thank You for loving us. Today, our prayer is the same as the words of that verse in the Psalms: "Search me, O God, and know my heart; try me, and know my anxieties; and see if there is any wicked way in me." Lord, test our thoughts, point out anything in us that makes you sad, and lead us along the path of everlasting life. Help us to release the control to You so Your blessed Son, who is within us and has become our life, can express Himself through us. We want to reflect Your glory and Your purposes to the world. Amen.

NOTES AND
PRAYER REQUESTS

Use this space to write any key points, questions, or prayer requests from this week's study.

Four Corrections Compelled by Adversity

IN THIS LESSON

Learning: How can I know if I am walking in God's will?

Growing: What happens if I get off course?

Have you ever been on a journey in which you needed to make a mid-course correction? Pilots make course corrections as they maneuver through air traffic and avoid potential storms. Road construction crews sometimes force us to make course corrections when we travel by car. The same holds true for life's journey. There are times when we need to make course corrections in order to arrive safely and soundly at our next spiritual destination and ultimately to heaven.

Adversity may be the detour, storm, or obstacle that compels us to make such corrections. The Lord always requires His beloved children to make changes in at least four areas. He insists that we: (1) conquer pride and humble ourselves to His will; (2) hate sin and purge ourselves of evil; (3) sift our friendships so they are in keeping with His plan for our lives; and (4) adjust our priorities so we place the highest value on the things of God and, in turn, adopt new habits of behavior based on right priorities.

Sometimes pride, sin, harmful relationships, and wrong priorities are so deeply embedded within us that we can hardly recognize them. That is a dangerous blindness. A primary reason to read our Bibles on a daily basis is to encounter God's direction. Any time you read your Bible, you should pray, "Show me, Lord, how this affects my life," or, "Reveal to me, Lord, how I need to change my life in order to conform to Your commandments and Your will."

We need to recognize the Lord corrects us *because He loves us*. Proverbs 3:12 is an important verse to memorize: "Whom the LORD loves He corrects, just as a father the son in whom he delights." A good parent guides a child's behavior—continually teaching the child what is good, acceptable, and beneficial, and what is bad, unacceptable, and harmful. If a parent doesn't do this for a child, the child grows up to be wild in behavior. In like manner, God wants us to be disciplined and mature adults in the faith so we can experience inner peace and harmony, enjoy relationships with other believers, and receive the blessings that God desires to give to us through other people.

Another reason the Lord corrects us is so we may be fruitful. Jesus taught this point using the analogy of a vine and its branches (see John 15:1–8). God, our heavenly Father, is the vinedresser. He prunes us—and will continue to prune us—so that everything in our lives bears fruit. Whatever He cuts away from our lives, even though it may involve the pain of adversity or trial, is for our benefit. It's dead wood as far as the Lord is concerned, and dead wood occupies space that could be occupied by fruit-bearing activities.

Furthermore, the Lord says we are His disciples when we abide in His Word and bear fruit. Just as the pruning of vines is important to their fruitfulness, so the Lord's correction is necessary for us to accomplish our God-given purpose in life and to find deep inner fulfillment. So, rather than shudder at the thought of the Lord's pruning, we should rejoice. We are about to be liberated of all dead weight and falsehood that may keep us from blessings.

1. When has God "pruned" your life? What did He cut away?

2. How did the pruning process feel while it was happening? What has grown into your life in place of what was cut off?

CORRECTING OUR ATTITUDE OF PRIDE

The Lord hates human pride. In James 4:6 we read, "God resists the proud, but gives grace to the humble." We find this same message three times in the Scriptures (see Proverbs 3:34 and 1 Peter 5:5.) Elsewhere, pride is listed among four things that the Lord hates: pride, arrogance, the evil way, and the perverse mouth (see Proverbs 8:13). In yet another passage, pride is listed among seven things that are an abomination to God (see Proverbs 6:17–19).

God hates pride so much because it is the one sin that keeps us from allowing God to use us for His purposes. When we are committed to doing things our way, we are not in a position to do things God's way. Pride renders us useless in the kingdom of God. We must always remember God does not exist for us. We exist for Him.

The Lord will not share His glory with anyone. When we take the glory for ourselves—saying, "Look at what I have accomplished!"—we deny that anything we accomplish comes about because God enables and empowers us to accomplish it. Any good in us is by His design and redemption. Anything noteworthy we become is because He wills it so. We have no goodness apart from God's goodness.

In Proverbs 16:18 we read, "Pride goes before destruction, and a haughty spirit before a fall." Not all destructions are caused by pride, but pride always ends in destruction. Usually, we lose the very thing we are the most proud about having achieved, earned, owned, or accomplished. Having pride is having too high an opinion about ourselves in relation to God and taking credit that belongs to Him. Having a haughty spirit is having too high an opinion of ourselves in relation to other people and taking credit that rightfully belongs to them.

When destructive adversity comes, it may be the result of your prideful behavior. If so, the Lord is permitting that adversity to point out your pride, to encourage you to humble yourself before Him (and perhaps before other people), and to submit to His will.

3. "By pride comes nothing but strife, but with the well-advised is wisdom" (Proverbs 13:10). When has your pride caused strife? How might humility have changed things?

4. What does it mean to be "well-advised"? How does good advice lead to wisdom rather than to adversity?

CORRECTING OUR ATTITUDE ABOUT SIN

Many people hope God grades on a bell curve—the kind of grading system often used in schools where a small percentage of students receive *A*s and *F*s, a larger percentage of students receive *B*s and *D*s, and the majority of students receive *C*s. The Scriptures tell us, however, that God doesn't play the averages. He is a God of absolutes. We are either evil or righteous, based on what we decide to do in response to Jesus Christ and His shed blood on the cross.

Our salvation is a matter not of works but of intentionally receiving Jesus Christ into our lives. As long as we shut the door to Christ, we are outside God's kingdom. He still loves us, He still calls to us, and His Holy Spirit still attempts to draw us to the Father—but we are not in a position to receive the benefits of being God's children. We are enemies of God, not heirs.

Those who hope God will tolerate a little sinfulness tend to tolerate sinfulness in themselves to the point they do nothing about their sin—even though they recognize it as sin. Now, you may be saying, "But we are all sinful. We all fall short of perfection." That is true. Paul says it plainly: "All have sinned and fall short of the glory of God" (Romans 3:23).

But recognizing we are sinful should compel us to do something about it. When we recognize we have sinned against God, we should not brush that aside casually as if to say, "Well, that's just my human nature." Rather, we need to come to God and say, "I have sinned. Have mercy on me. Change my human nature so I won't desire to do this again!" A recognition of evil should bring about a rebuke, a removal of evil, or a stand against evil. As Jesus told a woman who was caught in the act of blatant sin, we are to "go and sin no more" (John 8:11).

Facing the fact that we are sinful creatures is not the same as tolerating sin. The Scriptures teach that God wants us to hate sin and its consequences and turn away from evil at every opportunity. We are not to imitate evil. We are not to embrace evil. We are not to flirt with evil. We are not to be curious about evil. We are to turn our backs on it and run from it.

God wants us to flee from evil because He wants to protect us from sin's consequences. The Lord can look into the future and see what we will reap when we sow sinfulness. We have to recognize that we never receive only what we sow as a seed of sin. That seed produces a full harvest of sinful consequences—anguish, trials, heartaches, adversity. We will receive from our sinful deed a negative consequence with interest. Sinful seed multiplies just as good seed multiplies. Furthermore, sin *always* has negative consequences. Sin always bears its fruit.

The only antidote for sin is God's forgiveness. We can't work our way out of it or compensate for sin by good deeds. Only the shed blood of Jesus brings full remission of sins. The good news is that when we confess our sins to the Father, "He is faithful and just to forgive us our sins and to cleanse us from all unrighteousness" (1 John 1:9).

Sin will rob us of blessings. When a weed occupies a bit of ground, it keeps a fruitful plant from occupying that portion of the earth. The same goes for sin in our lives. As long as we give a safe harbor to sin, we keep ships from docking that are laden with God's blessing.

When adversity strikes, face the possibility that you may not have purged all evil from your life. Ask the Lord to give you the courage and ability to evaluate your ways, remove yourself from evil, and live a righteous life. It is possible. The Holy Spirit will enable you to do so if you ask for His help.

5. "He who covers his sins will not prosper, But whoever confesses and forsakes them will have mercy" (Proverbs 28:13). When have you tried to "cover" your sins? What was the result of your efforts?

6. Why are we commanded to confess and forsake sin, rather than just one or the other?

CORRECTING OUR ASSOCIATIONS

Adversity often brings us face to face with the fact we need to associate with different people. Perhaps we need new friends. Perhaps we need to sever ties with certain people. Perhaps we need to align ourselves more closely with Christian believers.

We were made for fellowship. None of us were designed to go it alone. But at times, we are unwise in the associations we make. We choose the wrong friends or partner or employee. Inevitably, the bad choice brings us adversity. The Scriptures provide a good model for true friendship in the lives of David and Jonathan. Jonathan's love for his friend David caused him to manifest these behaviors:

* He warned David of possible danger (see 1 Samuel 19:1–3).
* He spoke well of David, even to a person who considered David an enemy (see 19:4).

- He sought to do what David needed (see 20:4).
- He risked his life defending David (see 20:32–33).
- He helped David escape death (see 20:35–41).

Jonathan voiced one of the greatest statements of friendship in the Bible when he said to David, "Go in peace, since we have both sworn in the name of the LORD, saying, 'May the LORD be between you and me, and between your descendants and my descendants, forever'" (20:42). Now that's friendship!

Paul described Christian friendship in 1 Corinthians 13, what we have come to call the "love chapter." He described Christian love in these ways:

- Patient, kind, and humble (verse 4)
- Polite, selfless, unruffled, and positive (verse 5)
- Magnanimous and rooted in truth (verse 6)
- Supportive, hopeful, and enduring (verse 7)

Such love, Paul said, never fails. And such friendships do not create adversity. They are blessings in our lives, God's rich rewards to us on this earth. Bad associations, however, bring calamity. Evil associates attempt to turn us away from the Lord and His commandments. They are the friends, neighbors, relatives, or colleagues who say to us, "God didn't really say that," or, "God didn't really mean that," or, "God won't punish a person for doing that." Some go as far as to say, "You're special, so God won't require you to abstain from that." All of these lies are as old as the lie the serpent told in the Garden of Eden. We are to put away such friends from our lives and seek friends who desire to help us walk in God's ways.

True friends will stick with you in adversity, and they will stick with you all the way until God brings you to a better place in your life. Such friends are those who stick "closer than a brother" (Proverbs 18:24). True friends will be there for you when you need them.

7. "We command you, brethren, in the name of our Lord Jesus Christ, that you withdraw from every brother who walks disorderly" (2 Thessalonians 3:6). What does it mean to "walk disorderly"? Give specific examples.

8. Why are we commanded to "withdraw" from such people? How is this withdrawal carried out?

CORRECTING MISPLACED PRIORITIES

Adversity nearly always corrects our misplaced priorities. In times of adversity, we are reminded of what is truly important: our family and friends, our health, our peace of mind, our ability to experience all God has created, and our relationship with the Lord God.

Uzziah became the king over Judah at the age of sixteen. He sought God under the tutelage of Zechariah, and "as long as he sought the Lord, God made him prosper" (2 Chronicles 26:5). Uzziah accomplished great things during his reign. He defeated the Philistines, Arabians, Meunites, and Ammonites. He built fortified towers in Jerusalem and in the desert, where he also dug many wells. He built a strong army for the defense of Judah. His fame spread far and wide (see verses 6–15).

But then Uzziah no longer sought the Lord. The Scriptures tell us that "when he was strong his heart was lifted up, to his destruction" (2 Chronicles 26:16). He attempted to supersede the priests in the temple, and as a result he broke out with leprosy on his forehead, and he had leprosy until the day of his death. He dwelt in an isolated house and was cut off from the people of God and from the house of God.

Adversity can reveal that we are in danger of putting other things before the Lord. Any thing or person we put in the Lord's place is an idol—and the Lord gives no place to idols. He smashes them repeatedly throughout Scripture and calls them an abomination.

When adversity hits, the Lord may be trying to bring your priorities back into line. Ask Him to help you grow in understanding of how to realign your life in a way that will bring you peace, prosperity, and blessing. Ask Him to give you the courage to make different commitments and pursue habits that lead to godly righteousness and healthy relationships.

9. "Seek first the kingdom of God and His righteousness, and all these things shall be added to you" (Matthew 6:33). What does it mean to seek the kingdom of God? What does it mean to seek righteousness? Give examples of each.

10. Why does the Lord command us to "seek" these things? Why are they not automatically revealed and provided to Christians?

....

....

....

....

....

....

TODAY AND TOMORROW

Today: The Lord uses adversity to readjust
the course of my life.

Tomorrow: I will ask him to show me what
mid-course corrections he wants me to make.

CLOSING PRAYER

Heavenly Father, it is difficult to examine our lives. It is difficult to accept Your correction. But today, we ask that You would lead us to examine those areas where we know something is wrong—where we are dominated by self and have struggled time and again without securing the victory—and truly release those areas to You. Help us to see that surrendering our "rights" to You brings about the greatest freedom. In Jesus' name we pray. Amen.

NOTES AND PRAYER REQUESTS

Use this space to write any key points, questions, or prayer requests from this week's study.

WHAT ADVERSITY MAY REVEAL TO US

Learning: Am I supposed to learn something new about myself from adversity?

Growing: How can I gain from suffering?

As previously discussed, we are wise to engage in self-examination when adversity strikes. As we do, the Lord may lead us in a number of directions. Self-examination is not limited to areas of sinfulness or pride—it may involve areas of strength that we need to pursue. Some areas worthy of examination include:

- Our view of God
- The place of material possessions in our lives

- Our strengths and weaknesses
- Our unwillingness to forgive others
- Our faith in God

ADVERSITY REVEALS
OUR VIEW OF GOD

When adversity hits, how does it affect your view of God? Do you tend to see Him as a cruel taskmaster who is judging you unmercifully and requiring unreasonable behavior? Or do you regard Him as a benevolent Father who is permitting you to be chastened in a way that will result in your growth and perfection?

If your response is to feel that God is dealing with you unfairly or too harshly, don't deny your feelings. Instead, explore why you feel that way. In your self-examination on this point, you may discover that you have been taught incorrectly about God.

During my many years as a pastor, I have encountered hundreds of people who have a negative view of God. This is usually an opinion they have been taught by their parents, either directly or indirectly, and often it is based on their impression of their father. The Bible portrays our heavenly Father in these terms:

- Loving (see John 3:16; 1 John 4:8)
- Intimate (see John 15:15)
- Patient (see Psalm 103:8)
- Gentle and gracious (see Psalm 103:8)
- Generous (see Luke 6:38)
- Faithful and steadfast (see Lamentations 3:23)

If this is not your understanding of your heavenly Father, I encourage you to look up the references above and let the Word of God speak directly to you. Reread the Gospels. Read about Jesus, who said of Himself, "He who has seen Me has seen the Father" (John 14:9). Read closely what Jesus said about the Father. Let the Holy Spirit bring healing to you in this area.

At the opposite end of the spectrum, some people regard God as so loving that He would never do anything negative to His children. They believe God ultimately will overlook all their sins, as if they were of no account in His eyes. But as Paul wrote, "Do not be deceived, God is not mocked; for whatever a man sows, that he will also reap" (Galatians 6:7). God does not wink at sin, and neither should we. Sin is destructive and deadly.

The balanced view of God is that our heavenly Father is just, righteous, and absolute—and, at the same time, loving, generous, and available. His desire is to have warm and intimate fellowship with His children and to bless us, which is possible when we live in accordance with His laws and commandments.

Your response in adversity will reveal your opinion of God. Take note of your feelings and thoughts when adversity comes your way. Your understanding of the Lord and the relationship that He desires to have with you may be an area in which you need to grow.

1. "For the LORD loves justice, and does not forsake His saints; they are preserved forever, but the descendants of the wicked shall be cut off. The righteous shall inherit the land, and dwell in it forever" (Psalm 37:28-29). How can God both love His saints and "cut off" the wicked? How do you reconcile God's loving grace with His wrathful judgment?

2. What does it mean to be "preserved forever"? How does this concept tie in with adversity and chastisement?

_____

_____

_____

_____

_____

_____

_____

_____

_____

_____

ADVERSITY REVEALS OUR RELATIONSHIP TO THINGS

When adversity strikes, it reveals our materialism (or lack of it). Often we hear of people whose homes have been destroyed by fire, tornado, or flood, and their first response is, "We lost everything, but thank God we have our lives." In the end, what matters to us most is our health and safety and the health and safety of our loved ones. People count far more than things.

Yet in our world, many tend to use people and value things, rather than use things and value people. We are preoccupied with acquiring material possessions—in quantities far more than we need. We only need to take a look at the national debt, and the amount of personal debt of the citizens of our nation, to come to the conclusion that greed is rampant.

It takes adversity to call us back to our sense of values about what is truly important. The intangibles of love, hope, friendship, family togetherness, health, and peace of heart are far more valuable than anything that we can consume or put on a shelf to admire.

3. "The cares of this world, the deceitfulness of riches, and the desires for other things entering in choke the word, and it becomes unfruitful" (Mark 4:19). With what "cares of this world" do you struggle? How do they interfere in your relationship with God?

4. In what ways are riches deceitful? When have you been deceived by wealth or its pursuit?

ADVERSITY REVEALS OUR STRENGTHS OR WEAKNESSES

When adversity strikes, you find out what you are made of. You have probably heard people say in the aftermath of a crisis, "Before this happened to me, I never would have thought that I could deal with something like this. I didn't think I would have the strength."

In the Bible, God used adversity to help a man named Gideon understand the abilities that he possessed. The Israelites were being oppressed a group known as the Midianites, and God wanted Gideon to deliver His people from bondage. So he appeared to Gideon and said, "The LORD is with you, you mighty man of valor!" (Judges 6:12).

Gideon's automatic response was, "O my lord, if the LORD is with us, why then has all this happened to us? And where are all His miracles? . . . The LORD has forsaken us" (verse 13). Gideon saw himself and all the Israelites as weak and unworthy. The Lord responded almost as if He hadn't heard his words: "Go in this might of yours, and you shall save Israel from the hand of the Midianites. Have I not sent you?" (verse 14).

Gideon replied to God's charge with an extremely low view of himself: "O my Lord, how can I save Israel? Indeed my clan is the weakest in Manasseh, and I am the least in my father's house" (verse 15). Again the Lord encouraged Gideon, saying, "Surely I will be with you, and you shall defeat the Midianites as one man" (verse 16).

When the Lord calls you strong, don't proclaim that you are weak! When the Lord says you are forgiven, don't dwell on past sins! When the Lord calls you healed, don't dredge up past ailments! When the Lord says you are righteous, don't see yourself any other way!

On the other hand, you err if you see yourself as powerful in your own strength to the point you have no need of God. Never try to cope with an adversity on your own. You need the Lord's help. Adversity will bring home that lesson to you again and again. You cannot help yourself any more than Daniel could help himself in a den of lions or Peter could release himself from prison or Paul could save himself during a shipwreck.

The lesson, of course, is that you can't help yourself at *any* time. You need the Lord's help every hour of every day of every year if you are to live your life successfully—in spirit, mind, body, and in healthy relationships. He is your ever-present help.

It is important to come to the conclusion that your strength lies in the Lord and not in yourself. As Paul says, "The foolishness of God is wiser than men, and the weakness of God is stronger than men" (1 Corinthians 1:25). There is no comparison between God and humankind when it comes to wisdom and strength. When you rely on the Lord, you have access to His unlimited power and wisdom, and you will not end up in failure. But when you rely on yourself in adversity, you will fail and may even bring about more adversity.

5. "Fear not, for I am with you; be not dismayed, for I am your God. I will strengthen you, yes, I will help you, I will uphold you with My righteous right hand" (Isaiah 41:10). What does God promise in this verse when you are going through periods of adversity?

6. What are some practical ways that God has strengthened and encouraged you in times of trials and adversity in your life?

ADVERSITY REVEALS OUR UNWILLINGNESS TO FORGIVE

The Lord can have no part in sin, and He cannot ignore sin's presence. The Lord moves against sin continually and with the full force of His omnipotence. Only by the mercy of God are any of us spared. Those who believe in Jesus Christ and receive God's forgiveness are spared the wrath of God, even though they may be the beneficiaries of the Lord's chastisement and discipline.

Those who receive forgiveness from God are expected to extend forgiveness to others. And those who extend forgiveness to others are in a position to receive God's forgiveness. As Jesus said, "Whenever you stand praying, if you have anything against anyone, forgive him, that your Father in heaven may also forgive you your trespasses. But if you do not forgive, neither will your Father in heaven forgive your trespasses" (Mark 11:25–26).

Adversity sometimes reveals we have not forgiven others. In such cases, we must stand in our own sin and be subject to its consequences, which are never pleasant. Jesus told a parable to teach this lesson:

> There was a certain rich man who had a steward, and an accusation was brought to him that this man was wasting his goods. So he called him and said to him, "What is this I hear about you? Give an account of your stewardship, for you can no longer be steward."
>
> Then the steward said within himself, "What shall I do? For my master is taking the stewardship away from me. I cannot dig; I am ashamed to beg. I have resolved what to do, that when I am put out of the stewardship, they may receive me into their houses."
>
> So he called every one of his master's debtors to him, and said to the first, "How much do you owe my master?" And he said, "A hundred measures of oil." So he said to him, "Take your bill, and sit down quickly and write fifty." Then he said to another, "And how much do you owe?" So he said, "A hundred measures of wheat." And he said to him, "Take your bill, and write eighty." So the master commended the unjust steward because he had dealt shrewdly. For the sons of this world are more shrewd in their generation than the sons of light (Luke 16:1–8).

Jesus called this steward unjust, which he certainly was in his cheating and stealing from his master. Yet Jesus also noted the master commended him for his shrewdness. What did the servant do that was so shrewd? He forgave the debts of others to his own advantage. The Lord calls us to do the same—*not* to exercise poor stewardship, but to willingly forgive others. When we forgive those who have wronged us, we are able to receive forgiveness from the Father.

To fail to forgive is to harbor resentment, which can grow into bitterness, which in turn brings us into adverse relationships with others. To fail to forgive is also to harbor a desire for revenge—to make certain the person who has wronged us is punished according to our standards of what is right and wrong, or according to our standards of what is a fair punishment. The Bible teaches that we are to leave vengeance to the Lord and not take it on ourselves (see Romans 12:19). Any time we attempt to act as the judge, jury, and law for another person, we are in danger of being judged ourselves.

When you experience adversity, ask God to reveal whether you are in a state of unforgiveness toward someone. If you are, forgive that person and seek to make restitution. Then ask the Lord to forgive you and free you from any consequences of your unforgiveness.

7. "Judge not, and you shall not be judged. Condemn not, and you shall not be condemned. Forgive, and you will be forgiven" (Luke 6:37). What does it mean to judge another person? How is this different from recognizing a person's sin?

8. What does it mean to condemn another person? How is this different from acknowledging the consequences of sin?

ADVERSITY REVEALS OUR FAITH IN GOD

When hardships and trials come our way, we are wise to analyze the state of our faith in God. Is our first response, "God, I trust You to bring me through this and to work this to my eternal good"? Or is our response, "Oh, I'm doomed, and there is nothing that anybody can do"?

The storm on the Sea of Galilee served to teach Jesus' disciples this lesson. Jesus said to them, "Let us cross over to the other side" (Mark 4:35). The disciples should have taken that statement as a sure sign that Jesus expected to arrive safe and well on the other side of the shore. But then a great storm arose. The waves began to beat against the boat, and the boat began to take on water, and it was in apparent danger of capsizing.

Jesus was asleep on a pillow in the stern of the boat, oblivious to the storm in His faith that God had called Him to the other side of the lake and would ensure His safe arrival there. The disciples woke Jesus in their fear and said, "Teacher, do You not care that we are perishing?" (verse 38). How many times have we said the same thing to the Lord in our adversity? "Don't You care, Lord, that this is happening to me?"

Jesus arose, rebuked the wind, and said to the sea, "Peace, be still!" (verse 39). The wind ceased and there was a great calm. Then Jesus turned to His disciples and said, "Why are you so fearful? How is it that you have no faith?" (verse 40).

God has given each of us a measure of faith (see Romans 12:3), and He expects us to use our faith to overcome our fear. This is important because fear is always a component of adversity. A degree of fear is part of what makes a situation an adversity instead of just another experience. Fear is part of the negative dimension of adversity.

We generally fear an irreversible loss of some sort. We may fear a loss of life, limb, or sanity. In most cases, we fear things more subtle: loss of reputation, status, opportunity, or a relationship. Fear causes us to project the very worst that can happen—we will never recover, that all hope is lost, and that we will never enjoy something again.

Faith tells the opposite story. Faith says God is in control, and when He is in control, all things work together for our good (see Romans 8:28). Faith says that we will recover and our final state will be better than anything we have experienced thus far. Adversity may call our faith into question, but above all, it calls our faith to action. Adversity reveals areas in which our faith is weak and needs to grow. Adversity reveals areas in which we need to act in faith and not fear. When hard times come, we need to say to ourselves, "Now is the time to use my faith in a new way." The more we use our faith, the greater it grows.

Adversity acts in our lives as a mirror. It reveals the areas in which we need to improve, from God's viewpoint. So never waste an adversity. Learn all you can from each one. Truly, you can *advance through adversity* when you are willing to examine more closely the attributes in your life that are revealed in hard times.

9. "If any of you lacks wisdom, let him ask of God, who gives to all liberally and without reproach, and it will be given to him. But let him ask in faith, with no doubting, for he who doubts is like

a wave of the sea driven and tossed by the wind" (James 1:5–6). In what ways is a person who lacks faith similar to a wave of the sea that is driven and tossed by the wind?

10. "In this you greatly rejoice, though now for a little while, if need be, you have been grieved by various trials, that the genuineness of your faith, being much more precious than gold that perishes, though it is tested by fire, may be found to praise, honor, and glory at the revelation of Jesus Christ" (1 Peter 1:6–7). According to this passage, how do trials prove "the genuineness of your faith"? Why is this proof important?

TODAY AND TOMORROW

Today: God uses adversity to teach me important lessons and to make me stronger in Him.

Tomorrow: I will ask the Lord to help me make good use of adversity, rather than wasting it.

CLOSING PRAYER

Father, we don't like to accept what adversity reveals about the state of our heart—our view of You, the place we give material possessions, our weaknesses, our unwillingness to forgive, and our very faith in You. We pray that You would remove any bitterness within us toward You for allowing the adversity to happen in our lives—that You would melt our bitter hearts and help us see there is a way to rejoice in the midst of our distress. Help us to know that You can bring triumph, blessing, usefulness, and goodness out of even the most intense pain. Amen.

Notes and Prayer Requests

Use this space to write any key points, questions, or prayer requests from this week's study.

LESSONS PAUL LEARNED FROM ADVERSITY

IN THIS LESSON

Learning: Isn't my suffering unique?

Growing: How can I handle adversity
when I am feeling so alone?

I mentioned some of the adversity that Paul faced in in a previous lesson. In this lesson, I want to examine what Paul learned from his "thorn in the flesh." Again, we are not told specifically what Paul experienced, but the word for *thorn* that Paul uses in 2 Corinthians 12:7 refers to a sharp, pointed stake—not a little garden thistle. Paul endured intense pain and suffering.

Furthermore, Paul said the thorn was "a messenger of Satan to buffet me." The Greek word translated *buffet* is the same word (rendered *beat*) used to describe the ordeal Jesus went through in Mark 14:65: "Then some began to spit on Him, and to blindfold Him, and to *beat* Him, and to say to Him, 'Prophesy!' And the officers struck Him with the palms of their hands." Paul's thorn in the flesh included unrelenting anguish—a beating or pummeling.

Adversity comes to each of us in many packages and in varying degrees, but of one thing we can always be certain: the person who is experiencing adversity feels pain—perhaps not in a visible way, but always in an emotional, mental, or spiritual way. Paul's description of his experience reveals some principles about adversity we can apply to our lives:

- We should pray for deliverance in times of adversity.
- We must recognize we are not alone in our adversity.
- We need to trust in the Lord even when He doesn't remove the adversity.
- We can always rely on God's power to carry us through.

PRAY FOR DELIVERANCE

Paul asked the Lord to deliver him from his adversity. He recognized the Lord had permitted him to experience the thorn in the flesh for a good reason—so he would not be exalted above measure—yet he still pleaded with the Lord to free him from his pain. The Scriptures never scold us for praying for release from adversity. Jesus asked for release from an agonizing death even as He prayed in the Garden of Gethsemane (see Matthew 26:39).

We are wise to ask our heavenly Father to release us from the anguish of the adversity we are facing. Such a prayer is not wishful thinking. It is a statement of faith that we know God can release us and will release us from our anguish. Our release may not be immediate, but we can trust with certainty the Lord will answer our prayer in His way and in His timing.

1. When have you asked the Lord to release you from heartache, pain, or adversity? How did He answer that prayer?

2. What lessons have you learned in the past through adversity? What lessons might God be teaching you at present?

RECOGNIZE WE ARE NEVER ALONE

Paul recognized he was not alone in his adversity. He turned to the Lord and heard, "My grace is sufficient for you, for My strength is made perfect in weakness" (2 Corinthians 12:9). Paul had a keen awareness the Lord was with him in what he was experiencing.

What a comfort it is to know the Lord is with us and will never leave us! God's promise to His people through the ages has been, "I will not leave you nor forsake you" (Joshua 1:5). Jesus promised His disciples, "Lo, I am with you always, even to the end of the age" (Matthew 28:20). No matter what we are going through today, the Lord is with us. He will not abandon us in our troubles, even though we may feel the Lord is silent.

Often we get frustrated when we go through adversity and the Lord doesn't speak to us as He did to Paul. We may find ourselves saying, "Where is God?" However, we must be aware that even though God may not be speaking to us, He is *with* us. Silence is not to be equated with inactivity. God is moving behind the scenes in ways we cannot know with our senses.

When God is silent, we have only one reasonable option: to trust Him, wait on Him, and believe He is at work on our behalf. God may be *quiet*, but He has not *quit*.

3. "Let your conduct be without covetousness; be content with such things as you have. For He Himself has said, "I will never leave you nor forsake you" (Hebrews 13:5). When have you felt God had abandoned you? What is required of you to believe His promise in this verse?

....
....
....
....
....
....
....

4. Why does the writer of Hebrews mention covetousness in this connection? What does coveting have to do with adversity?

....
....
....
....
....
....
....

TRUST IN THE LORD

Paul had to face the fact that God was not going to remove the adversity. At no time did Paul claim that God was going to heal him of the thorn in the flesh. The Lord made it plain to Paul that He heard him plead three times for release, but the Lord was not going to give him either release or relief. Rather, He was going to give him peace.

What a difficult realization that must have been for Paul! He was a man of great faith, a man who brought deliverance and healing to many, a man obviously beloved by God and by believers throughout the Greek world—and God was not going to release him from an obviously painful affliction. Many Christians experience similar situations. A physician tells them a disease is terminal, or they realize a relationship is not going to be reconciled, or they face some other situation that will not turn out as they hoped. Sometimes God answers our prayers by saying "no," and when that happens, discouragement and despair can set in. But we need to remember the Lord's words to Paul: "My grace is sufficient for you."

The Lord may not remove our problem, but He is going to compensate us fully for it. In whatever ways we are weak, He is going to be strong. He will fill in the crevices of our pain and discouragement with His presence. What we aren't, He will be. What we can't do, He will do. The Lord says His grace *is* sufficient—not *was* sufficient, not *will be* sufficient. Trusting God is a moment-by-moment and day-by-day experience. As we trust God, He imparts His grace. What He did for Paul, He will do for you and me.

The psalmist said, "God is our refuge and strength, a very present help in trouble" (Psalm 46:1). A "very present help" does not mean God will act immediately to eliminate the cause of our trouble; rather, it means that the Lord is "very present" to help us. He is intimately connected to us and is inseparably linked to our problem. He is present! The psalmist goes on to say in verses 2–3 that because God is our refuge, strength, and very present help:

Therefore we will not fear,
Even though the earth be removed,
And though the mountains be carried into the midst
    of the sea;
Though its waters roar and be troubled,
Though the mountains shake with its swelling.

Most people who experience an earthquake or violent storm at sea have moments of terror. And yet, the psalmist declares we can have great peace of heart and mind when we know God is with us in our trouble and will never abandon us. Our confidence is in the fact the "LORD of hosts is with us" (verse 7).

5. When have you realized the Lord was not going to deliver you from the anguish of a problem? In what ways did you see God was walking with you?

6. When have you become aware of God's presence in your own life or in someone else's life? How can the words of Psalm 46 encourage you during times of trial?

RELY ON GOD'S POWER

Finally, Paul discovered that God's power reaches its peak at the lowest point of adversity. He wrote, "Therefore I take pleasure in infirmities, in reproaches, in needs, in persecutions, in distresses, for Christ's sake. For when I am weak, then I am strong" (2 Corinthians 12:10). Paul was saying he learned through the experience that, when he allowed the grace of the Lord to be sufficient in his weakness, he was actually stronger as a result.

Consider for a moment a person who tinkers with the engine of an old car, gives up, and finally sells his "bucket of bolts" to a master mechanic. The master mechanic pulls out the old engine and replaces it with a completely rebuilt one, which gives great speed and power to the old car. People see the vehicle on the streets with its out-of-date, nearly antique chassis and say, "Who would have thought an old worn-out car like that could have such zip?" Well, it's not the chassis that changed but the source of power under the hood. That was what Paul was saying about his life. The weaker he was, the more he was energized by God's presence and power—and, therefore, the stronger he was.

There is no pleasure to be derived from infirmities, reproaches, or persecutions. But if we believe God's grace is manifested in our lives through adversity, then we can take joy in that fact. The spiritual blessings received from the Lord during a time of adversity will overshadow the pain caused by the adversity itself. The pain caused by adversity is limited—it may seem all-encompassing, but it is limited in both scope and time. The spiritual blessings the Lord offers are unlimited. They surpass all understanding and extend beyond time into eternity.

If the Lord does not remove adversity from our lives, He will enable us to live with it triumphantly and with an inner peace that is beyond reason. The greater the adversity, the more the glory of the Lord shines through the situation.

7. "Therefore I take pleasure in infirmities, in reproaches, in needs, in persecutions, in distresses, for Christ's sake. For when I am weak, then I am strong" (2 Corinthians 12:10). In what exactly was Paul taking pleasure? Was he pleased by the adversity, or by some result of it? Explain.

8. In practical terms, how can you take pleasure even in times of pain? What part does your thinking play in this process?

GOD FILLS OUR WEAKNESSES

Paul said with boldness that he gladly boasted of his infirmities because it was in them that "the power of Christ" rested on him (2 Corinthians 12:9). Paul was not ashamed he had a thorn in the flesh. He was not embarrassed the Lord had not delivered him from it. He did not hide his infirmity from the Corinthians. At the same time, he didn't boast about his infirmities to get their sympathy or make them think he was somehow special. Paul continually pointed toward Christ, who made his infirmity bearable and who made his infirmity a part of his witness.

We are wise to follow Paul's example. Our weaknesses are not something about which we should be ashamed. Neither are they something about which we should lay claim as if to say, "I'm disadvantaged in this way, so the Lord *has* to take care of me." Rather, our witness is this: "Just look what the Lord can do! Here I am, in dire straits [or in great turmoil or in great pain], and see how good and how great our God is!"

Over the years, I've experienced some incredibly painful moments in my life personally. At the same time, God has blessed In Touch Ministries in ways that are almost beyond my comprehension. In the natural world, a person would say, "That can't be. A leader needs to be strong and powerful in all areas of his life for the organization to grow and excel." I give witness to the contrary. In my hours of greatest weakness, God has shown Himself to be strong. He is accomplishing what He wants to accomplish, not because of *my* strength, but because I have allowed *His* strength to fill my weakness.

As the hymn "To God Be the Glory" declares:

To God be the glory, great things He hath done,
So loved He the world that He gave us His Son,
Who yielded His life our redemption to win,
And opened the life-gate that all may go in.
Praise the Lord, praise the Lord,
Let the earth hear His voice!
Praise the Lord, praise the Lord,
Let the people rejoice!
Oh, come to the Father, through Jesus the Son,
And give Him the glory; great things He hath done.

To God be the glory . . . great things He has done! What God did for Paul—and what the Lord has done for me—He will do for you when you experience adversity that threatens to level you on the inside. He will raise you up, by His power and in His power.

9. "Rejoice always, pray without ceasing, in everything give thanks; for this is the will of God in Christ Jesus for you" (1 Thessalonians 5:16–18). In practical terms, how does a person rejoice during times of suffering? How did Paul do it? Explain.

10. Why does Paul say, "*in* everything give thanks," rather than "*for* everything give thanks"? What do you think is the difference between those two statements?

TODAY AND TOMORROW

Today: I am never alone, not even when my
life seems the darkest.

Tomorrow: I will trust the Lord in adversity,
even when He does not remove the pain.

CLOSING PRAYER

Father, thank You for loving us and for not answering all of our requests with which we petition You because we don't want to suffer here and we don't want to suffer there. Thank You for listening to us and not scolding us—not making us feel guilty or being angry with us—but just lovingly reminding us of what You reminded Paul: "My grace is sufficient." I pray for those who have not discovered Your love and indeed feel "buffeted" by life, that they might receive Jesus Christ as their Savior and their Lord. I pray that You will show them how to live victoriously by coming to You in complete surrender. Thank You that when we are weak, You are strong. Amen.

NOTES AND
PRAYER REQUESTS

Use this space to write any key points, questions, or prayer requests from this week's study.

ADVANCING THROUGH ADVERSITY

IN THIS LESSON

Learning: What does it really mean to "advance through adversity"?

Growing: How can I profit from adversity?

The theme of this entire study has been how we can *advance* through adversity. But to what do we advance? What is the end to which we should aspire as we are going through times of anguish, heartache, or trial? In this lesson, we will deal specifically with three goals we can pursue during times of adversity. I phrase them here as prayers:

- "Lord, purify and enlarge my faith as the result of this time of trouble."

- "Lord, give me greater compassion for others, especially those who do not know You, as the result of this adversity."
- "Lord, use this adversity in my life to prepare me to minister comfort, encouragement, and Your Word to others."

We can pray these prayers with confidence, because the Lord desires to answer each of them with a resounding "yes."

ADVANCING TO GREATER AND PURER FAITH

When workers want to refine a precious metal, such as gold or silver, they first heat it to extremely high temperatures so it becomes liquid. Anything that is an impurity, or dross, floats to the top of the cauldron. The dross is skimmed away, leaving the metal pure and nearly translucent. Only when the metal is pure do the workers pour it into molds, where it cools and becomes bullion, rare and precious. The Lord uses adversity in a similar way in our lives to purify our faith. He wants us to have both a perfect and a proven faith.

Faith can be viewed in two ways—by quantity and by quality. Faith is frequently described in the Bible by quantity: little, great, or perfect. *Little faith* says, "God can do it, but He may not." *Great faith* says, "God can do it, and He will do it." *Perfect faith* says, "God said that He would do it, so it is already done." When we have perfect faith, we have absolutely no doubt that God is God in every moment and in every circumstance of our lives. We are truly living by His Word, trusting in Him to fulfill every detail of His Word in our lives.

Faith also has three types of quality: inherited, textbook, and proven. *Inherited* faith is faith we have received from a parent or a pastor. We believe faith works because we have seen it work in the lives of others. We believe in Christ Jesus because others have believed. We acknowledge God's Word as real and potent because we have seen it lived out and working in the lives of those we trust.

Paul reminded Timothy that his faith dwelt first in his grandmother Lois and his mother Eunice (see 2 Timothy 1:5). Timothy had grown up in the faith.

Textbook faith is Bible-book faith. It is faith that is mostly mental. We read what the Bible says and declare, "I believe that is true. What the Bible says is the truth of God for humankind." We believe the stories we read in the Bible. We believe that Paul and the other writers are telling us the truth in the books and letters that are part of the Old and New Testaments. We believe in God because, as the old gospel song says, "the Bible tells us so."

Both inherited faith and textbook faith are important to have. We benefit greatly from growing up in families in which a love of God is nourished and the Bible is taught. We grow in faith from reading the Word of God and hearing sermons based on the Bible. But the third type of faith, proven faith, is the most important.

We demonstrate *proven faith* when we test the principles of the Bible for ourselves in times of adversity. This is the type of faith described in 1 Peter 1:6–7: "Now for a little while . . . you have been grieved by various trials, that the genuineness of your faith . . . may be found to praise, honor, and glory at the revelation of Jesus Christ." When we use our faith in times of adversity, we can trust God to give us greater faith—in other words, to grow our faith toward perfect faith. And we can be assured that we are acquiring proven faith.

Elijah had a proven faith in God. God sent him to the Brook Cherith, and Elijah obeyed. There by the brook, the Lord fed him with bread and meat brought to him by ravens. No doubt Elijah came to count on the birds to show up in the morning and the evening with his daily ration from God. Elijah had his needs met, with sufficient food to eat and water to drink.

But then the brook dried up. The word of the Lord came again to Elijah, "Arise, go to Zarephath." Elijah obeyed. There in Zarephath, a widow made a cake for him from her last oil and flour, and God provided a miracle so that her jar of oil and bin of flour did not run out. She continued to feed herself, her son, and Elijah from the unending source until the famine ended and food was available once again. Elijah had experienced the provision of the Lord and was able to proclaim to the widow that God was going to provide for her, regardless of what her circumstances told her. That is faith—knowing that God is going to fulfill His Word and care for His children, regardless of the severity of a situation (see 1 Kings 17.)

How does adversity purify our faith? *First, our faith is valuable not because we possess faith but because of Christ Jesus, who is the object of our faith.* The object of our faith defines our faith. He is pure, and the quality that He gives to our faith is purity.

Second, adversity strips everything from us but Christ. In times of adversity, we realize that nothing else satisfies but Jesus Christ and nothing is secure except Christ's presence in our lives. The money in which we trust may be lost. The friends in which we place our faith may desert us. The house in which we feel secure may go up in flames. When all has been stripped away by adversity, we see clearly that Jesus Christ remains. He alone is utterly and eternally steadfast.

Proven faith endures because it is based on our personal knowledge and experience that God endures. God wants us to have a pure, perfect, and proven faith. Therefore, He will answer "yes" when we pray, "Lord, purify and enlarge and prove my faith as the result of my going through this time of trouble."

1. "We also glory in tribulations, knowing that tribulation produces perseverance; and perseverance, character; and character, hope" (Romans 5:3–4). Why can we "glory" in our tribulations?

2. What is the refining process that Paul describes in this passage as it relates to our faith?

....

....

....

....

....

ADVANCING TO GREATER COMPASSION

Adversity can give us a special kinship of spirit with others and cause us to have a greater compassion for them. When we are struck with pain, we are amazed at how many other people have experienced that same pain—pain to which we might have been blind in the past.

Many people have shared with me how they never felt much sympathy for those who had gone through a divorce when they felt secure and happy in their marriage. But when their marriage disintegrated, they found they had much greater compassion for those individuals. The same is true for those with sickness: the person who has the most compassion for someone diagnosed with a life-threatening ailment probably has, or has conquered, that same disease. I know I relate to others in a more understanding way as a result of my own experiences in these areas.

We may *want* to have greater empathy for people in certain circumstances, but we rarely *will* have great empathy unless we have been touched by the same problem. Certainly, as believers in Christ, we can have this empathy for those who don't know the Lord in a personal way. We have been delivered from the anguish and adversity wrought by sin. How much more should we be able to feel for those who are still living in sin—and desire to intercede in prayer for them, reach out in love to them, and share the gospel of Christ with them! Adversity either hardens us or softens us. If we let it harden us, we are subject to more adversity. If we allow it to soften us, it can lead us to advance in our compassion for others.

The Lord wanted Jeremiah to learn this lesson. He said, "Arise and go down to the potter's house, and there I will cause you to hear My words" (18:2). So Jeremiah went down to the potter's house, and there he found a potter making something at his wheel. The vessel the potter made of clay was marred in some way, so he crushed the clay back into the turn of the wheel and began to remake it into another vessel, one that seemed good to him. God said to Jeremiah, "O house of Israel, can I not do with you as this potter? . . . Look, as the clay is in the potter's hand, so are you in My hand, O house of Israel!" (verse 6).

The Lord desires to see certain traits in us to the point He will work and rework us as clay in His hands until we manifest those traits He desires. Compassion for others is one trait. Compassion gives rise to patience, generosity, kindness, and actions rooted in love. Compassion moved Jesus to heal people and give them words of life-giving blessing. Compassion moves us to rescue people from evil and turn them to Jesus Christ, the source of all that is good.

Let adversity work the good work of compassion. Have confidence the Lord will always answer "yes" to the prayer, "Lord, give me greater compassion for others, especially those who do not know You."

3. "Be of one mind, having compassion for one another; love as brothers, be tenderhearted, be courteous; not returning evil for evil or reviling for reviling, but on the contrary blessing, knowing that you were called to this, that you may inherit a blessing" (1 Peter 3:8–9). What does being *compassionate* and *tenderhearted* mean to you?

4. What does it mean to be *courteous?* What does it mean to *bless* others? Give a practical example of each.

5. When have you returned evil for evil? When have you returned a blessing to someone who reviled you? What were the results?

ADVANCING TO A NEW DIMENSION OF MINISTRY

Adversity prepares us in unique ways for ministry. God wants each of us to be involved in the ministry of comforting others. But it is a very poor comforter who has never needed comfort. Adversity equips us to minister to others as nothing else can.

There was a time in my life when I gave little comfort to those who were going through hard times emotionally. A big part of me believed that if people would just confess their sin, they could find peace of mind and live happily ever after. All that changed when I went through hard times emotionally in my own life. I now can feel the hurt of a man or woman who sits in my office and cries. I can identify with those who desperately seek change in their lives but don't know where to begin. I can relate to those who are frustrated and yet are unable to pinpoint the nature of their hurts. I know better how to comfort them, even as I counsel them.

There is a difference between our ability to minister the Word of God to people and our ability to minister to people. To minister the Word of God, we need to know the Bible and see how it applies to various situations. But we need more than a knowledge of the Word if our ministry is to be received by a person. To minister to people, we need proven faith, compassion, and an ability to empathize with their feelings, if not their exact situation. As we have already discussed in this lesson, proven faith and compassion are derived to a great extent from adversity. Adversity prepares us to minister to people, to comfort and encourage them, and to build them up to trust God, to believe God's Word, and to expect God's best.

To comfort others is to impart strength and hope to them. By strength, I mean Christ's strength. Our goal as comforters is to move people from relying on their own strength to that of Christ Jesus. Every time I read the biography of a great saint, I am encouraged by God's grace to that person during times of adversity and difficulty. I come away thinking, "If God sustained that individual through such trials, He will sustain me as well." The person's testimony imparts strength to me and motivates me to go forward rather than to give up.

To impart hope is to enable others to take their focus off their immediate circumstances and place it on eternal things. We will not completely understand much of our suffering until we see Jesus. But we have the hope we will see Him and He will tie all the loose ends of our lives together in a way that makes sense.

Paul described this hope in 2 Corinthians 4:16-18: "Therefore we do not lose heart. Even though our outward man is perishing, yet the inward man is being renewed day by day. For our light affliction, which is but for a moment, is working for us a far more exceeding and eternal weight of glory, while we do not look at the things which are seen, but at the things which are not seen. For the things which are seen are temporary, but the things which are not seen are eternal."

Keep in mind it was only after the disciples had been through the adversity of their Lord's crucifixion and resurrection that Jesus said, "Go therefore and make disciples of all the nations, baptizing them in the name of the Father and of the Son and of the Holy Spirit, teaching them to observe all things that I have commanded you; and lo, I am with you always, even to the end of the age" (Matthew 28:19–20).

When we come through adversity with stronger faith and greater compassion, we soon find people to whom we can minister both strength and hope. In so doing, we find an enlarged purpose for our lives and a deeper feeling of inner satisfaction that we are being used by God to fulfill His plan on the earth. The Lord always answers "yes" to the prayer, "Lord, use this adversity in my life to prepare me to minister comfort, encouragement, and Your Word to others."

6. "Rejoice with those who rejoice, and weep with those who weep. Be of the same mind toward one another. Do not set your mind on high things, but associate with the humble. Do not be wise in your own opinion" (Romans 12:15–16). What does it mean to "set your mind on high things"? What is the opposite of this?

7. What does it mean to be "wise in your own opinion"? How is this related to weeping with those who weep?

8. How have the past experiences in your life qualified you for ministry to others?

....

....

....

....

....

....

ADVANCING TO
MATURITY IN CHRIST

A spiritually maturing Christian is one who is advancing in faith toward a perfect, proven, and pure faith and is able to share the Word of God with others in a way that is applicable to their life's needs and circumstances. That person is advancing in compassion for others, to a new level of ministry, and is truly able to comfort those who are in trouble, sickness, or any kind of need. Adversity compels us to grow in Christ if we trust in Him in the midst of our trials and tribulations and avail ourselves of the opportunity to learn and grow from them.

9. "Be sober, be vigilant; because your adversary the devil walks about like a roaring lion, seeking whom he may devour. Resist him, steadfast in the faith, knowing that the same sufferings are experienced by your brotherhood in the world" (1 Peter 5:8–9). What does it mean to be sober and vigilant in the face of adversity?

....

....

....

....

....

....

10. How do we resist the devil? What does this resistance have to do with sufferings?

_____

_____

_____

_____

_____

TODAY AND TOMORROW

Today: Adversity can grow my faith and give me greater compassion for others.

Tomorrow: I will ask the Lord to use adversity to make me more profitable to His kingdom.

CLOSING PRAYER

Heavenly Father, purify and enlarge our faith as the result of the adversity we are facing. Give us compassion for others, especially for those who do not know You, as the result of the trials we face. Use the adversity we confront in our lives to prepare us to minister comfort, encouragement, and Your Word to others. We want to be available vessels—stepping-stones of Your love—to help those who are suffering in their adversity. We want to help them understand the wonderful work You are doing in their lives so they can become enriched, blessed, and even profit from that adversity. In Jesus' name we pray. Amen.

NOTES AND PRAYER REQUESTS

Use this space to write any key points, questions, or prayer requests from this week's study.

COURAGE IN TIMES OF ADVERSITY

IN THIS LESSON

Learning: What am I to do when I am feeling overwhelmed with my problems?

Growing: How can I face adversity and still serve God?

In many ways, a time of adversity is like boot camp: it is rigorous, painful, and challenging. Adversity causes us to adopt new routines and habits, to develop aspects of our being—physical, mental, emotional, or spiritual—that might have been undeveloped previously. Adversity sometimes puts us under the authority of people who affect our lives in ways that are foreign to us. In all these areas, we need courage to keep our balance as we feel hit by so many new feelings, limitations, challenges, and advice.

We must have the courage to face and endure times of adversity and to make the necessary changes in our lives that our trials and hardships compel us to make. In either case, we can trust the Holy Spirit to help us grow and change so we follow the example set by Jesus Christ.

Joshua knew about adversity. Forty years of wandering in the wilderness had qualified him to understand hardship, trials, and troubles—physical, relational, spiritual, emotional, and mental. Joshua also knew that the Lord was with him and that He was with the people. He had been a close associate of Moses and had grown in his faith and leadership abilities under him.

So when the time came for the people of God to cross the Jordan River and inhabit the land of promise, the Lord named Joshua the leader to succeed Moses. He said to Joshua, "Arise, go over this Jordan, you and all this people, to the land which I am giving to them—the children of Israel" (Joshua 1:2).

God then spoke to Joshua three times about the need to have courage, saying, "Be strong and of good *courage*, for to this people you shall divide as an inheritance the land which I swore to their fathers to give them. Only be strong and very *courageous*, that you may observe to do according to all the law which Moses My servant commanded you. . . . Have I not commanded you? Be strong and of good *courage*; do not be afraid, nor be dismayed, for the LORD your God is with you wherever you go" (verses 6-7, 9).

Note in this passage that God required Joshua to have:

- Courage to make decisions that would affect people under his leadership
- Courage to keep His laws and commandments, even as changes were occurring
- Courage to remember continually that the Lord was with him, in spite of what the circumstances might indicate to the contrary

We need courage in the same three areas of our lives as we face adversity.

REACHING OUT TO OTHERS TAKES COURAGE

We need God's wisdom to know how to deal with people. Our times of adversity and heartache always involve the people we love. For this reason, we need courage to get beyond our pain and help our children, our parents, our spouse, our associates, and others to cope with the pain they are experiencing. It takes tremendous inner fortitude when we are sick, facing a loss, or in emotional turmoil to get beyond ourselves—to put aside our inner hurt and frustration—and be concerned about others. Yet that is precisely what the Lord calls us to do.

In fact, it is by getting outside ourselves and helping others in need that we often find the strength to get through adversity. Time and again, I've watched people who were going through hard times reach out to help those who were hurting just as much as they were. I have seen them benefit not from what they *received* from others but from what they *gave* to others. This principle of God defies human reasoning, but it is absolutely true in God's kingdom.

In Luke 6:38, Jesus tells us, "Give, and it will be given to you: good measure, pressed down, shaken together, and running over will be put into your bosom. For with the same measure that you use, it will be measured back to you." We assume that when we give we will have less than we had before. But in God's eyes, when we give, we receive a blessing—both materially and spiritually.

It is when you think you have nothing to give that you need to give! It takes courage to do so, but the Lord promises to give you the courage when that moment arrives. So ask Him to help you, to guide you, and to show you the people to whom you should give. Ask Him to reveal the best gift possible, in the best timing, and for the best results.

1. "He who is greatest among you, let him be as the younger, and he who governs as he who serves. For who is greater, he who sits at the table, or he who serves? Is it not he who sits at the table? Yet I am among you as the One who serves" (Luke 22:26–27). What does it mean to "be as the younger"? To be a person who serves at a banquet?

2. How did Jesus demonstrate these principles? How can you imitate Him and follow His example?

KEEPING GOD'S LAWS
REQUIRES COURAGE

Adversity can knock us off stride. Often, our routines or our locations will change during a time of adversity. A flood may force us from home. An illness may force a change in work habits. A break in a relationship may force us to alter our normal routines. Life can be tumultuous at times.

We need courage to stay true to God's Word and live according to His commandments—especially when we confront discouragement, disappointment, or despair in the aftermath of adversity. Our loss or pain may lead us to think, "What's the use? Why live a godly life if this is what happens to Christians?" But remember the Lord doesn't promise us success and ease in this life. He promises us His presence and His eternal rewards.

Time and again in the law of Moses, we find the word *keep*. The Israelites were commanded to keep the feasts, to keep the law and commandments, to keep the Sabbath day holy, to keep the ordinances, to keep their oaths to God, to keep themselves from evil, to keep God's judgments. "To keep" means to hold fast and to cherish at the same time. When adversity strikes, that should be our mindset: above all else, we need to hold fast to the Lord and cherish our relationship with Him. Rather than blame God or turn from God, we need to turn to God and rely on His help to get us through our challenging times.

Moses said to the children of Israel, "Therefore keep the words of this covenant, and do them, that you may prosper in all that you do" (Deuteronomy 29:9). Keeping God's laws in the face of adversity actually leads us toward prosperity—which is a better state of being. King David gave this same advice to his son Solomon as part of his final blessing: "You will prosper, if you take care to fulfill the statutes and judgments with which the Lord charged Moses concerning Israel. Be strong and of good courage; do not fear nor be dismayed" (1 Chronicles 22:13).

When adversity hits you, those around you may criticize you for clinging to your faith or reaffirming your belief that God is a good and benevolent heavenly Father. They may mock you or scorn you. Don't be dismayed if that happens. Continue to keep God's Word and be faithful in your relationship with the Lord. Ask the Lord to give you courage to withstand the hurtful comments of others and to be able to give a bold witness about God's power and presence even in your time of trouble.

3. "I would have lost heart, unless I had believed that I would see the goodness of the LORD In the land of the living. Wait on the LORD; be of good courage, and He shall strengthen your heart; wait, I say, on the LORD!" (Psalm 27:13–14). What does it mean to "wait on the Lord"? Give some practical examples.

4. Why does God command us to "be of good courage"? What part do our choices and our actions play in gaining courage?

5. What are some ways you have continued to trust in God during times of adversity?

_____

_____

_____

_____

_____

_____

_____

_____

_____

_____

COURAGE TO HOPE AND TO BELIEVE

In times of adversity, things can seem so bleak and so dark that we find ourselves on the verge of giving up hope. Others may foretell doom and encourage us to face what they see as inevitable. Job's wife was one such person. Job was covered with painful boils from the soles of his feet to the crown of his head, and she said to him, "Do you still hold fast to your integrity? Curse God and die!" (Job 2:9). Job responded, "You speak as one of the foolish women speaks. Shall we indeed accept good from God, and shall we not accept adversity?" The Scriptures add, "In all this Job did not sin with his lips" (verse 10).

When we are faced with negative circumstances and then negative comments from others, we need courage to continue to stay positive—to continue to believe the Lord is with us! Hope and faith are not automatic responses in times of hardship and trial. They require an exercise of the will, bolstered with courage. At times, we must say aloud to ourselves, "I know that God will bring me through this. I know God is a good and loving Father, and He is doing a good and eternal work in my life." If no one else speaks hope, we need to speak it to ourselves.

Part of the need for courage also may reside in the need to withstand the enemies who are moving against us—in other words, those who are causing our adversity. Moses realized that would be the case for Joshua and the Israelites, and he said to them, "Be strong and of good courage, do not fear nor be afraid of them; for the Lord your God, He is the One who goes with you. He will not leave you nor forsake you" (Deuteronomy 31:6).

It takes courage to continue to believe in God and to have hope in His power over our enemies while they are pummeling us into the ground. Goliath no doubt found David's claims about the greatness of God to be ludicrous as he stood in the Valley of Elah and watched a stick of a lad run toward him. But at the end of the day, David had victory in his hand and joy in his heart (see 1 Samuel 17).

So today, ask the Lord to give you courage to continue to believe in Him and in His presence with you as you go through adversity. Ask Him to renew your hope and faith. He will honor your request.

6. In 2 Chronicles 19:1 we read, "Behave courageously, and the Lord will be with the good." What part does behavior play in finding courage? How can our behavior lead to cowardice?

....

....

....

....

....

7. Why does the Lord say He will be with His people if they behave courageously? How can a lack of courage lead us away from God?

....

....

....

....

....

COURAGE TO BE LIKE JESUS

We must think of Jesus when we consider what it means to have courage to help others in spite of intense persecution, to keep God's laws and commandments in spite of great temptation, and to never stop believing in the Father even in in the darkest hours of anguish. Jesus was a man of courage. He trusted the Father to give Him courage, and He exercised that courage in fulfilling the Father's will for His life. He is our supreme example.

God glorifies Himself in us and through us so we might be saved and so we might reflect His life on this earth. He wants us to be conformed to His likeness so that others will want to know more about the love of God and the power of God in us when they see us helping people, declaring the truth of His Word, and trusting in Him in spite of our adversity. When we are courageous to do what the Lord commands us to do, we truly are His witnesses because we reflect His presence in the world.

Your life has a purpose far beyond comfort, ease, or pleasure. God wants to use you to fulfill His very purposes on this earth. So take courage today, regardless of what you might be facing. God will give you the courage when you ask Him for it. He will honor your courage in remaining true to Him and His Word and in giving to others out of your need. A wonderful blessing is in store for the courageous!

8. "Do not be overcome by evil, but overcome evil with good" (Romans 12:21). What does it mean to be "overcome by evil"? How does this happen in life?

9. "Therefore whoever confesses Me before men, him I will also confess before My Father who is in heaven. But whoever denies Me before men, him I will also deny before My Father who is in heaven" (Matthew 10:32–33). What does it mean to confess Jesus before other people? When might a person be called to do this?

10. What does it mean to have Jesus deny you before the Father? What does this imply concerning the importance of *not* denying Him?

TODAY AND TOMORROW

Today: Courage is gained by acting in faith; it is a choice, not an emotion.

Tomorrow: I will follow the example of Christ, God's own man of courage.

CLOSING PRAYER

Lord, thank You for loving us and for giving us such a beautiful example in the life of Jesus Christ of how to bravely face adversity. We know that He understood and experienced trials like no other person on the face of this earth, and there is so much we can gain from His model to us. As we face trials and difficult situations, may we respond with submission, commitment, and surrender. May we allow You to build into our lives that beauty, power, and authority that will make us into mighty vessels for Your glory. We pray this in Jesus' name and for His sake. Amen.

NOTES AND
PRAYER REQUESTS

Use this space to write any key points, questions, or prayer requests from this week's study.

OUR RESPONSE TO ADVERSITY

IN THIS LESSON

Learning: How do I know if adversity is caused by God or my own sin?

Growing: What should I do, practically speaking, when adversity strikes?

As we have seen in this study, no one can avoid adversity completely. The winds of adversity blow in all directions. The certain fact is that we *will* have adversity in our lives. However, each of us has the power to choose our response to adversity. We have it within the power of our will to determine how we will face adversity and how we will behave during times of adversity.

We must realize the most vital outcome of adversity is the formation of our character. This outcome is eternal and is most important to our heavenly Father. Material possessions may be restored, relationships may be reconciled, the body may be healed, but all these solutions are temporary. What happens to us on the inside will count forever.

Our response to adversity must thus be intentional. If we just go with the flow, we will not grow. In fact, we may be weakened or destroyed if we merely respond at a superficial or an emotional level—if we place blame on others, have a pity party, become bitter, adopt a spirit of revenge, are hateful or resentful, or become disillusioned about life and God. In the end, if we do not reverse these patterns, we can get into terrible trouble—because each of these behaviors leads us to turn from God and refuse to trust Him with our lives.

If we refuse to benefit from adversity, we actually choose to be destroyed by it. If we give in to the negative downward spiral that adversity can create, we find the adversity multiplies (growing ever more negative and painful), is prolonged, and becomes more destructive—especially to our Christian witness.

Adversity that we allow to go unchecked and unmediated by the Lord will only lead to more adversity. We will lose ground rather than advance if we fail to learn and grow during life's toughest times. So, when adversity hits, we must make a decision that we will, with God's help, come through our time of hardship better, not bitter. We must choose to burrow into our relationship with God rather than ignore or blame God and cast aside our faith. We must choose to do the hard work of self-examination rather than live in denial and blame others or the devil. This intentional approach to adversity takes courage. But this is the only way that we will ever advance in our spiritual walk.

You response to adversity will fall into one of two categories. The first type of response will be necessary if the adversity you are facing is caused by your own sin. The second type of response will be necessary if the adversity is coming from Satan, as permitted by God.

THE RESPONSE TO ADVERSITY CAUSED BY SIN

As you examine your life, if you conclude that sin is at the root of your adversity, there are five important steps you must take. *First, you need to accept responsibility for what you have done or left undone.* Some sins will be the result of your action, while others will be the result of what you should have done. Both result in negative consequences. You must acknowledge you own part of the problem in which you find yourself.

Second, once you have faced up to your sin, you must confess it to God. You need to go to your heavenly Father and admit to Him that you know you have sinned, that you are truly sorry for doing so (and not merely sorry you have been caught), and that you desire His forgiveness. No matter what you have done, you can be assured that when you ask the Lord to forgive you, He will do so. As long as you still have a conscience and an awareness that you have sinned before the Father, you are a candidate for God's forgiveness. He grants that forgiveness freely, based on the price Jesus Christ paid on the cross for your redemption. You cannot earn God's forgiveness. You can only accept it.

Third, once you have received forgiveness from God, you must forgive yourself. Refuse to wallow in the memories of your pain and self-recrimination. Make a decision to move forward in your life with the freedom that has been given to you by God to embrace His ways and His righteousness.

Part of this move forward may involve making amends or seeking reconciliation with another person. If so, take action quickly. Once you have asked forgiveness and made amends, refuse to live in the past or dredge up your past sin in future conversations with that individual. Live a new life before the person that you wronged or were associated with in your sin. Adopt a new way of relating to that person so both of you live in righteousness.

If the other person rejects your request for forgiveness, or if the other person refuses to live according to God's plan, recognize that you have done all that God requires you to do. Move forward in your life and refuse to be held back by another person's disobedience to the Father.

Fourth, in moving forward, you must choose to pursue God's will for your life. This is at the heart of repentance, which literally means to turn around as an act of your will. You must make new decisions to live in a way that is pleasing to God and not in the way that was a part of your past sin. You need to then follow through on those decisions that you have made.

Fifth, as you move forward with God's grace and by the power of the Holy Spirit working in you, you need to choose to respond positively to your adversity. Refuse to give in to complaining or whining about the challenging situation that you are facing. Choose instead to respond positively in these ways:

- Take a long, hard look at your life and search out ways in which you may become a stronger and more positive person (especially in areas where you have been weak or negative in your thinking).
- Accept your adversity as a lesson from God intended to teach you what *not* to do in the future.
- Thank God for loving you enough to not allow you to get by with your sin and face more dire circumstances.

When you respond to sin-related adversity in these ways, you should feel cleaner, stronger, and better than you have ever felt before! You will have great freedom in your spirit and joy in your step. Indeed, you will have *advanced* in your spiritual walk. If you do not feel this way after confessing your sin to God, making amends, and moving forward in your life, reassess which of these five steps you might not have completed.

1. "Search me, O God, and know my heart; try me, and know my anxieties; and see if there is any wicked way in me, and lead me in the way everlasting" (Psalm 139:23–24). How, in practical terms, does a person examine himself spiritually?

2. What should we do if God shows us a "wicked way" that is in our lives?

3. What is "the way everlasting"? What part does self-examination play in this?

4. How do you feel when you recognize that you have sinned? How do you feel after you confess your sin to God and you receive His forgiveness?

5. Have you ever asked forgiveness of another person and not received it? What did you do? What was the outcome?

THE RESPONSE TO ADVERSITY PERMITTED BY GOD

As we noted in a previous lesson in this study, there will be times when God will allow the enemy to bring adversity in your life. If you are not a believer in Christ Jesus, you must either deal with the adversity as if it is a consequence of your sin, or you must establish a relationship with your heavenly Father so you will have the full benefit of His help in your crisis. In fact, God might have allowed adversity for this precise purpose: so you would turn to Him and place your trust in Jesus Christ as your Savior.

However, if you are a believer in Christ Jesus, you need to take the following ten steps when responding to adversity that is coming from Satan, as permitted by God. *The first step is to reaffirm your relationship with God.* You may want to review the steps listed in the previous section of this lesson, "The Response to Adversity Caused by Sin," as a reinforcement to your own heart and mind that you are in right standing before the Father and that Jesus Christ is the Lord of your life.

Second, pray for removal of the adversity. Ask others to join with you in praying that God might deliver you from the troubles besetting you. Recognize your willingness to pray may be the very lesson the Lord has for the adversity in your life: to get you to trust Him enough to ask Him to remove the difficult circumstances. Pray, "Deliver me, Lord, and give me a heart of thanksgiving for the good work that You are going to do."

Third, yield to God's timetable for removal of the adversity. Not all adversity is reversed instantaneously, but all adversity is reversed inevitably. So be patient and allow God to do His full work in your life and the lives of others who may be involved. Don't rush to judgment or try to fix things apart from God's directives.

Fourth, reaffirm God's promise of sustaining grace. Say to the Lord, "I trust that You are with me and that You will carry me through this ordeal to the glory of Your name and to my eternal benefit. I rely on Your strength and presence to get me through this time of trouble." You may find it helpful to recite aloud verses of Scripture in which God promises to heal, deliver, restore, and reward His faithful people. You may also find it helpful to meet periodically with others who will encourage you to trust God as you move through your circumstance.

Fifth, resist any temptation to sin or to deny God. Such temptation is a direct satanic attack on your life. The Word of God states that you are to "resist" the enemy, and when you do so, he will flee from you (James 4:7).

Sixth, begin to explore ways in which you might grow through this experience. A godly counselor may be helpful to you. Face up to areas of weakness in your life, and review what you might do to become stronger in these areas.

Seventh, deal with your adversaries in a godly way. Jesus taught, "Love your enemies, bless those who curse you, do good to those who hate you, and pray for those who spitefully use you and persecute you" (Matthew 5:44). To *love* means to give. You cannot love others without giving to them. So give something positive to your enemies who may be trying to take something from you. Speak well of those who speak ill of you. Pray for those who are out to do you harm. Recognize those who do ill to you as a child of God are not *of* God; rather, they operate as Satan's messengers. They are doing Satan's work for him. You must hate Satan, not his messengers. When you treat your enemies with love, offer words of blessing to them, and pray for them, you neutralize those individuals. Satan no longer can work through them.

Eighth, read passages in Scripture in which people encountered adversity. Be encouraged by the way in which God brought them through their adversity with victory.

Ninth, reflect on ways in which you might minister to others in your adversity. Comfort others, help others, and give to others. Turn yourself outward.

Tenth, ask the Lord to give you courage as you stand strong in faith, give to others in need, and remain true to your relationship with Him.

These ten steps are for advancing in your spiritual life. As you look back through them, you will see that you don't need adversity to grow in these ways. Adversity serves as a crash course to compel you to grow in the Lord. God is in the process of building you, of creating you, of making you into one of His saints on the earth. So yield to that process. Rejoice that He is forming you into the very likeness of Christ Jesus.

Ultimately, your response to adversity is to say to your heavenly Father, "Have Your way in my life." Adversity brings you to your knees.

While you are on your knees, acknowledge Jesus as Lord and humble yourself before the Father so He can do His good work in you.

6. "When you pray, say: Our Father in heaven, Hallowed be Your name. Your kingdom come. Your will be done On earth as it is in heaven. Give us day by day our daily bread. And forgive us our sins, For we also forgive everyone who is indebted to us. And do not lead us into temptation, But deliver us from the evil one" (Luke 11:2–4). What are the things we are to ask from God?

7. What are each of the things that we are to do ourselves?

8. How do these two lists pertain to dealing with adversity?

9. "Submit to God. Resist the devil and he will flee from you" (James 4:7). What is involved in submitting to God? In resisting the devil?

10. How do these things pertain to adversity?

TODAY AND TOMORROW

Today: All adversity is allowed in my life by God in order to make me more like His Son.

Tomorrow: I will seek God's face diligently when adversity strikes.

CLOSING PRAYER

Father, we thank You and praise You in Jesus' name. We bless You and honor You for who You are—the loving, gracious, omnipotent, omniscient God in whose presence all of us dwell twenty-four hours of every single day. Today, we ask You in Jesus' name for those who are lost, for those whose lives are tormented with adversity, that by faith they would trust in You as their personal Lord and Savior. We pray they would come to You, asking for the forgiveness of their sin, and trust in Your sacrificial atoning death for the payment of their sin by saying "yes" to You today. And Lord, we pray that You would continue to shape our response as we experience adversity and trials in our own lives. Amen.

Notes and Prayer Requests

Use this space to write any key points, questions, or prayer requests from this week's study.

THANKSGIVING IN THE MIDST OF ADVERSITY

IN THIS LESSON

Learning: Am I really supposed to give thanks for the suffering in my life?

Growing: How can I use gratitude and thanksgiving to connect with God in the midst of suffering?

We've seen throughout this study that all people experience adversity, including those who follow Christ—maybe even *especially* those who follow Christ. However, we don't have to be passive in our experiences with adversity. We don't have to simply let it wash over us and hope it goes away quickly. Instead, we are called to actively and intentionally respond when we face trials and tribulations in this life, because doing so brings glory to God.

In this lesson, we are going to examine a secret weapon that can super-charge our response to adversity as disciples of the Lord Jesus Christ. Now, the bad news is that this secret weapon isn't something we typically think about or reach out for when we experience trials. But the good news is that this weapon is not only powerful but also freely available in an unlimited supply for any who choose to access it.

This secret weapon is thanksgiving. It's gratitude. And it's a critical piece of our arsenal as we seek to advance through adversity in service to our God.

IN EVERYTHING GIVE THANKS TO THE LORD

We noted previously that the apostle Paul knew a thing or two about adversity. In fact, he experienced extreme levels of adversity on several occasions throughout his ministry and mission to preach the gospel. But Paul knew a lot about thanksgiving as well. In 1 Thessalonians 5:16–18, he wrote several surprising commands we should take seriously:

> Rejoice always, pray without ceasing, in everything give thanks; for this is the will of God in Christ Jesus for you.

Those are three relatively small verses, but they certainly carry some weight in terms of their content. "Rejoice always." That's not very easy, is it? "Pray without ceasing." That's not easy, either! But the third command can feel particularly difficult to obey, especially when we are dealing with adversity: "in everything give thanks."

Perhaps you feel a little incredulous as you read those words. Maybe a little confused. "Give thanks in everything?" But there's no doubt that is what Paul commanded us to do through the inspiration of the Holy Spirit. We know that because it's not the only time he commanded us to do it. In Ephesians 5:20, he wrote we are to be "giving thanks always for all things to God the Father in the name of our Lord Jesus Christ."

In everything, give thanks. Give thanks always for all things. Take a moment to think about what those words really mean.

Now, this is one of those places where a non-believer might come in contact with God's Word and think, "This is why I can never be a Christian. I could never give thanks for everything that has happened in my life." So, let me offer a little clarification on what these verses mean.

Here's the truth: we can never—and should never—give thanks for something that goes against God's character. We should never express gratitude or thanksgiving for a situation that is contrary to who He is. Therefore, when we experience something such as a broken arm or other sickness and we're in terrible pain, we don't give thanks for that pain. When we're dealing with loneliness, sadness, or pressure, we don't give thanks for those emotions. And when we slip up and fall into a period of sin, we don't give thanks for that sin.

How, then, can we obey Paul's commands to give thanks in everything? By choosing in all circumstances to express thanksgiving to God for His *goodness*—by giving thanks that Jesus is our Savior, our Lord, and our God. No matter what happens—no matter our pain, difficult emotions, or even our sin—we can say, "Lord, I don't understand why You allowed this to happen, but in the midst of this, I'm going to give You thanks because I know You'll help me survive. I know You'll help me bear the pain. I'm going to thank You because You'll be with me in the middle of it."

So, we don't give thanks because bad things are happening to us. We don't give thanks for the adversity itself. But we give thanks because we believe, in the words of Paul, that "all things work together for good to those who love God, to those who are the called according to His purpose" (Romans 8:28).

1. Which of Paul's commands in 1 Thessalonians 5:16–18—"rejoice always," "pray without ceasing, "in everything give thanks"—is the most challenging for you? Why?

....

....

....

....

....

....

....

....

....

2. When, how, and how often do you express thanks to God?

....

....

....

....

....

....

....

....

....

....

GIVING THANKS KEEPS US AWARE OF GOD'S PRESENCE

We often wonder, "What is God's will for my life?" One thing we can say for sure is that it's God's will for us to express thanksgiving in all circumstances. It's God's will for us to give thanks, and to do it now—not when the adversity finally goes away. Giving thanks provides blessings in our lives, especially when we are in the midst of adversity. In the remainder of this lesson, we'll explore four additional reasons why we should be grateful in all things, beginning with the first: giving thanks keeps us aware of God's presence, which contributes to a godly life.

Giving thanks to our heavenly Father in everything reminds us that we're not walking alone. Whatever we may hurt over, whatever we may weep over, whatever may cause us to suffer loss, we can know this: God is with us. We're not enduring it alone. If there's one thing we need when we're going through adversity, it's the presence of our almighty Creator.

Now, here's the really wonderful truth: the more that we are aware of God's presence in our lives, the more that we will grow in godliness. When we are aware of God's presence, it becomes much more natural for us to look at things from His point of view. *How does God see this? What has God promised me in the midst of this? How is He going to work in this situation?*

In addition, by choosing to express thanksgiving to God even in adversity, we become more aware of the incredible promises He's given us through His Word. For example, we remember that He's promised to never leave us or forsake us (see Deuteronomy 31:6). We remember that nothing can separate us from the love of Christ (see Romans 8:38–39).

If you still feeling uncertain about the power of gratitude, try a simple exercise. Tomorrow morning, as soon as you wake up and start your day, take just a few moments to pray and to thank God for the fact that before you have even taken your first step, you are walking in His presence. Thank God for the fact that no matter what happens to you during that day, it will happen in the presence of an all-loving, all-powerful, all-knowing, ever-present, and perfectly holy God.

What could be finer than that?

3. "You will show me the path of life; in Your presence is fullness of joy" (Psalm 16:11). How have you experienced God's presence in recent weeks? How has that brought joy?

_____

_____

_____

_____

_____

_____

_____

4. "So shall My word be that goes forth from My mouth; it shall not return to Me void, but it shall accomplish what I please" (Isaiah 55:11). What are some promises from God's Word that have been proven true in your life?

_____

_____

_____

_____

_____

_____

_____

_____

_____

GIVING THANKS MOTIVATES US TO SEE GOD'S PURPOSES

The second reason we should give thanks during adversity is that being grateful motivates us to look for God's plan and God's purposes in everything that happens to us.

All of us have times in our lives where we think, "God, what are you up to?" All of us have times when we don't understand the circumstances or the situations we're experiencing. We don't understand the reasons behind it, and we may even wonder if there is any reason. We ask, "Is what's happening to me accidental or random?"

In those moments, we need to remind ourselves of some basic truths about God. Namely, that He is sovereign over all things. That means everything that happens in your life and mine—God is aware of it. More than that, He's in control of it. He could change things if He wanted. He could have made it so you never experienced that adversity, or He could have pulled you out of that trial long ago.

Why is that important? Because the fact that God did not steer you away from that adversity or bring an end to it more quickly means *everything is going according to His plan.* God knows when you experience adversity, and so you can have confidence there is a purpose behind whatever circumstance you are going through.

Oftentimes we are so shocked by adversity that all we can think about is getting out—all we can think about is getting comfortable again. *God, why are You allowing this? God, what can I do to make this end?* But when we remember to be thankful even in the midst of pain, when we remember to give thanks, we are reminded that God has a plan for our lives. And that plan without a doubt includes whatever adversity we are experiencing at this particular moment.

God has not forgotten you. Nor will He ever forget you. Therefore, be grateful even when you go through trials, because there's a purpose behind it. Remember, as Paul wrote in Romans 8:28, "And we know that all things work together for good to those who love God, to those who are the called according to His purpose."

The only one who can make that promise is the Almighty God of the universe. With that in mind, you can say, "God, I don't understand what's happening right now. I don't like it. It's painful. But even so, I'm going to trust You because You are a loving God. I'm going to thank you in spite of everything I feel."

5. What can you say for certain about God's plan for your life?

6. In what areas are you finding it difficult to trust God? Why?

GIVING THANKS EMPOWERS US TO REJOICE

Giving thanks during adversity allows us to rejoice in the middle of that adversity. In fact, thanksgiving fuels and empowers our ability to rejoice, which in itself is another great antidote to adversity.

Here's what I mean. The pain and suffering that you are presently going through may be so deep, so penetrating, and so exhausting that when you try to tell God you're grateful, you don't feel it. You're just expressing words. How does God feel about that? He understands. He knows how you feel, and He knows how you would *like* to feel. The wonderful thing about our loving God is that when you can't even express what you would like to express, He hears it.

When your pain shouts out louder than you can speak, He still hears you, even though nobody else can.

So, what should you do when you don't *feel* grateful or thankful? You should continue to express your gratitude. You should keep giving thanks to God—and you should do it again and again. "God, I know that You are good, and I thank You for that goodness even though I don't understand what is happening in my life right now." "God, I know You love me, and I thank You for that love." "God, I thank You for my salvation."

As you continue to express your gratitude, all of a sudden you will realize, "My goodness—I do feel grateful!" The act of expressing thanks will lead you to feeling thankful and will even give you the ability to rejoice in the middle of that adversity. This is not because of you or any strength you have, but because of the Holy Spirit living inside of you. And it's the same process: you start rejoicing with your lips. And the more you praise God and rejoice even in the darkest times, the more you start to rejoice with your heart. With your soul. With your very being.

Gratitude leads to rejoicing, and rejoicing is another powerful weapon as we strive to advance through adversity.

7. "Praise Him with the sound of the trumpet; praise Him with the lute and harp! Praise Him with the timbrel and dance; praise Him with stringed instruments and flutes! Praise Him with loud cymbals; praise Him with clashing cymbals! Let everything that has breath praise the Lord" (Psalm 150:3–6). What are some of your favorite ways to praise God?

8. In Philippians 4:4, Paul says, "Rejoice in the Lord always. Again I will say, rejoice!" How does that verse intersect with Paul's instructions in 1 Thessalonians 5:16–18?

....

....

....

....

....

....

....

Giving Thanks Energizes Us for Each Day

Finally, there is something important that happens to us when we give thanks to God each day, and especially when we express gratitude during difficult times. It energizes us. It strengthens us. It changes us not only physically but also emotionally and spiritually.

Now, when I say thanksgiving energizes us physically, that's exactly what I mean. I know there are lots of energy drinks and caffeinated products out there—seems like more and more each day. I don't have any idea whether those work the way they claim, but I do know what happens when we intentionally make a habit of expressing thanks to God. It recharges us. It energizes us.

That makes sense when you think about the nature of pain, suffering, hurt, disappointment, and unbelief. Why? Because they drain us. Negative emotions and negative circumstances rob us not only of our joy and peace but also of our physical energy. But when we trust the Lord and look to Him—when we come before Him with gratitude in our hearts—it is as if He refills our tanks.

Remember the words of the prophet Isaiah:

He gives power to the weak,
And to those who have no might He increases strength.
Even the youths shall faint and be weary,
And the young men shall utterly fall,
But those who wait on the LORD
Shall renew their strength;
They shall mount up with wings like eagles,
They shall run and not be weary,
They shall walk and not faint (40:29–31).

You just feel different when you bring gratitude into your life. You can walk farther. You can run longer. You can do more. You think differently. You rejoice more. You can sing. There's just something wonderful that happens when you are able to thank God and praise Him even when nothing around you looks like it's worth thanking and praising Him for.

And remember: if you're feeling a little skeptical about this idea, that's okay. But be sure to try it. Take some time each day to praise God and thank Him, even during those days that are tough—especially during those days that are tough. You'll see that what I'm saying is true. And you'll be all the more thankful because of it.

9. When have you felt especially energized or empowered by a spiritual experience?

10. What steps can you take to make gratitude and thanksgiving a part of each day?

....

....

....

....

....

....

....

....

....

....

....

....

NEVER OUT OF REACH

I don't know where you are in life. But I do know this: you're not anywhere beyond the reach of a caring Father who loves you enough to send His only begotten Son, Jesus, to die on the cross for you. Whenever you think God doesn't care, think about the cross—that's God's declaration to the world, "I love you, I love you, I love you; and this is the way to eternal life."

He is willing to forgive you of your sins no matter what you've done. He's willing to turn your life around. He is willing to turn the worst kind of bitterness and resentment and hostility toward God into something fantastic. But only after you surrender your life to Him.

And He is both willing and able to carry you through even the worst seasons of adversity and suffering and pain. He can do it, and He will do it. You can help that process when you use the secret weapon of thanksgiving.

TODAY AND TOMORROW

Today: God acknowledges my desire to express gratitude in Him, even when my feelings don't match my words.

Tomorrow: I will actively and intentionally express thanks and rejoice this week during a moment of adversity.

CLOSING PRAYER

Thank You, dear God, that You don't remove the adversity from our lives until You have completely accomplished Your purpose within us. Help us today, Lord, to reconsider our response to adversity. Help us to give thanks that You are continually using the trials that come in our lives to make us more aware of Your presence and to see Your purposes. Empower us to rejoice in all things and energize us for each day. Remind us that adversity is the greatest motivation for our spiritual growth—and the greatest means of conforming us to Your likeness. Amen.

NOTES AND
PRAYER REQUESTS

Use this space to write any key points, questions, or prayer requests from this week's study.

GRACE TO KEEP GOING

IN THIS LESSON

Learning: Is it okay for me to quit and walk away from adversity that God has allowed in my life?

Growing: How can I benefit from God's grace during troubles and trials?

One of the values in which many of us like to take pride is the refusal to quit. We make motivational posters for our offices and post slogans about perseverance online: "Never give up!" We put athletes on a pedestal when they power through an injury rather than throwing in the towel. And we look back through history for military leaders we can turn into heroes because they refused to surrender, even to the point of death.

Notice I said we tend to take pride in the *value* of refusing to quit—in that *idea*. I didn't say we take pride in refusing to quit *ourselves*.

The reality is we often choose to quit. We quit our New Year's resolutions (usually around the third week of January). We quit our Bible-reading plans, our jobs, and our relationships. In fact, just like everyone else in the world, we have the capacity to quit just about anything if it gets hard enough or even inconvenient enough.

As we wrap up this study on advancing through adversity, it's important that we talk about this topic of quitting. Why? Because when you go through a difficult circumstance, there will come a time when you are ready to quit. It will happen. Even if you follow every instruction and insight you have read throughout this study, you will still feel the desire to quit when you are faced with adversity.

When that moment comes, you will be forced to make a choice: to quit, or to keep going. As we'll see in this final lesson, the only truly effective way to keep going in those moments is to rely on God's grace.

HIS GRACE IS SUFFICIENT

How do we keep going in the face of adversity? That's the question we need to address together in this final lesson. In order to do that, we're going to look back at a Scripture passage we've already visited in an earlier portion of the study. We dipped our toes into 2 Corinthians 12:7-10 before, but now we're going to dive all the way in:

> And lest I should be exalted above measure by the abundance of the revelations, a thorn in the flesh was given to me, a messenger of Satan to buffet me, lest I be exalted above measure. Concerning this thing I pleaded with the Lord three times that it might depart from me. And He said to me, "My grace is sufficient for you, for My strength is made perfect in weakness." Therefore most gladly I will rather boast in my infirmities, that the power of Christ may rest upon me.

142

Therefore I take pleasure in infirmities, in reproaches, in needs, in persecutions, in distresses, for Christ's sake. For when I am weak, then I am strong.

Take a moment to think about Paul. Think about everything he had accomplished for God's kingdom. Think about all the disciples he mentored. Think about how much of the New Testament he wrote through the inspiration of the Holy Spirit. Now imagine the apostle Paul, this giant of the faith, down on his knees in prayer and just begging God to remove this thorn in his flesh. Three times he prayed about it. "Lord, please take this way." "Lord, please take it." "Lord—please, please, please remove this from me."

But then look at God's answer: "My grace is sufficient for you."

If you're scoring at home, that is a "no." This is one of those times when God directly answered the prayer of His child to say, "No, I am not going to give you what you're asking. Why? "My grace is sufficient for you, and my strength is made perfect in weakness."

What kind of answer is that from a loving God? What kind of answer is that to a servant who had relentlessly, at great personal cost, given everything for the sake of the gospel? If there was ever a moment when Paul thought about giving up, this might have been it.

1. "Concerning this thing I pleaded with the Lord three times that it might depart from me" (2 Corinthians 12:8). Are you currently feeling "weak" or in distress about some aspect of your life? How can you relate to the situation that Paul was facing?

2. "But by the grace of God I am what I am, and His grace toward me was not in vain" (1 Corinthians 15:10). How has God's grace proven to be "enough" in your life?

....

....

....

....

OUR UNDERSTANDING OF GRACE

The reality of Paul's situation is that God had perfect knowledge of where he was and what he needed. You might recall that Paul wrote in Philippians 4:19 that he knew his God would supply all his needs according to His riches in glory in Christ Jesus. Isn't it interesting how we can use that verse so quickly when it comes to money and finances? But then, when the bottom drops out and we're hurting and in pain and suffering and feeling helpless and hopeless, somehow that verse doesn't seem to ring true anymore.

Perhaps the reason it doesn't feel true is because we don't understand grace. *What is this grace of God all about? What does it mean that His "grace is sufficient" for us?* To begin, grace is God's goodness and kindness directed toward us. He extends it to us without regard to any merit—it's not something we deserve. In fact, we receive God's grace in spite of what we deserve.

Furthermore, the idea that God's grace is "sufficient" means it empowers us in whatever we need moment by moment in our specific circumstances. In other words, God's grace is His provision for us at the point and at the moment of our need. How much provision? *Sufficient*—which is to say, adequate, complete, overflowing, and abounding. God is not cheap. You and I have never come to Him and seen Him give us *almost* enough. God says His grace will provide everything we need at our moment of need.

But here's the really wonderful news: this is a universal promise from our God. It wasn't given only to Paul. God gave that promise for the church—not just the Corinthian church but the *entire* church, which includes all who have believed in Christ for salvation. This is a promise given to every single child of God.

No matter the magnitude of the adversity you are facing, God says He will be there at the point of your need. He will make you adequate, sufficient, complete, and enable you to walk through that trial. He will empower you to not give up, not quit, not walk away, not throw in the towel, and not throw away your faith. Because of His grace, you can keep going.

3. What are some points of need that you are feeling sharply in your life today?

4. When have you experienced God's grace and provision in an unexpected way?

GOD'S GRACE MEANS WE SHOULD NEVER QUIT

In light of God's promise to us, we are going to use the remainder of this lesson to examine three specific truths we need to remember about God's grace. The first is that because God is committed to showering us with His grace at the point of our need, we can never justify giving up and quitting in the face of adversity. Certainly, that's what we want to do at times. We think, "God doesn't expect me to put up with this. I'm gone." We throw in the towel and walk away.

But that is never okay, because God has promised to meet our needs. His grace is sufficient, and His strength is made perfect in our weakness. In His sovereignty and perfect knowledge, we can know that if He has allowed us to experience a season of adversity, there's a reason for it. Thus, we must not quit in the midst of it.

Maybe you are thinking, "Why would God do that? Why would God intentionally bring us into adversity? Why wouldn't He get us out of it as quickly as possible?" One reason is that we learn our greatest lessons during the most difficult trials. After all, how many spiritual lessons have you *really* learned when you had sufficient money, a nice house, good clothes, a nice car, and everybody just loved you to death? How much have you ever learned in that kind of comfort?

Probably not much. But how much did you learn when the bottom suddenly dropped out and forced you to fall on your face before Almighty God, crying out to Him and asking Him to help see you through? How much have you learned when you had no other choice but to rely on Him for strength? For sufficiency? It's in those moments we begin to learn something about God we didn't know before. We learn about His love for us in a way we never felt before.

Here is something else we need to remember: when adversity strikes, God doesn't necessarily want us to be delivered. That doesn't mean He won't deliver us from some things. But oftentimes God wants us to see the thing causing us difficulty is not a tyrant in our lives. It can actually be a servant. It can produce a blessing and a reward. How? Because His grace is sufficient.

When you face adversity, God doesn't want you to sink beneath it all. He wants you to rise above it. That is why it's critical for you to never quit. When you say, "I give up, I'm walking away, and

I don't have to put up with this anymore," what you are doing is allowing adversity to take you down.

The alternative is for you to get your focus on God and allow Him to raise you above it all. And when you do that, He will absolutely transform your life in the process.

5. "If we endure, we shall also reign with Him. If we deny Him, He also will deny us" (2 Timothy 2:12). What does it mean to *endure* under trials? What promise are we given in this passage for enduring for the sake of Christ?

....

....

....

....

....

6. What does it look like on a practical level for a person to "quit" in the middle of adversity? What are some spiritual lessons or truths about God you have learned in recent months as a result of your perseverance?

....

....

....

....

GOD'S GRACE PRODUCES CONFIDENCE IN US

The second thing grace does in our lives is this: it ignites a spirit of confidence in us. It helps us say, "You know what? I'm going to trust God even though I'm going through this. God is going to take me through this and bring me to a place of victory no matter what."

Peter experienced this in an amazing way. Do you remember what happened on the night Jesus was arrested by the religious authorities? Three times Peter denied even knowing His Lord. He was rattled and afraid, and so he disassociated himself from his Savior. Then, when he realized what he had done, the Bible says he wept bitterly.

Of course, Jesus knew this was going to happen. In fact, Jesus *told* Peter that it was going to happen. But there's something very interesting that Jesus said during that moment in the upper room when He predicted Peter's failure: "But I have prayed for you, that your faith should not fail; and when you have returned to Me, strengthen your brethren'" (Luke 22:32).

Do you see the grace overflowing in this moment? Jesus knew Peter was about to deny Him. Even so, Jesus prayed that Peter would be strengthened through that moment of adversity so his faith would not fail—so he would not *quit* during the difficult period after.

That's the grace of Jesus. That's unmerited favor.

Can you imagine the confidence Peter experienced when everything came full circle and he received forgiveness from Jesus? Can you see how Jesus' grace ignited and empowered Peter to persevere through any difficulty—even up to his own death for the sake of Christ?

You can hear Peter's confidence when you read his epistles, including this passage: "Beloved, do not think it strange concerning the fiery trial which is to try you, as though some strange thing happened to you; but rejoice to the extent that you partake of Christ's sufferings, that when His glory is revealed, you may also be glad with exceeding joy" (1 Peter 4:12–13).

7. What reasons do you have today for your confidence in Christ?

8. What are some steps Christians can take to intentionally access confidence and joy in the midst of adversity?

....

....

....

....

....

GOD'S GRACE KEEPS OUR EYES ON THE FATHER

The third benefit we receive from God's grace in the face of adversity is that it keeps pointing us to the Father. Grace helps us get our eyes off the trouble, the heartache, the problem, the thorn. It helps us focus our eyes on the sovereign Creator of this universe. Grace keeps pointing us to God and to the truth that He has a reason and a purpose and a plan for allowing adversity.

Now, maybe you are thinking, "But you don't know what I've been through." I'm sure I don't. But I can say this: I've lived long enough and been through enough in my life to know that what God says is always true—that if He has promised it, it is going to happen. God doesn't spout off things in the Bible to give us a little empty encouragement. No, His grace is a practical, down-to-earth, Monday-morning kind of grace. It works—no matter when, where, what, why, or who.

But how does it work? For starters, grace is there to remind you that God is going to bring you through this circumstance, whatever you are facing. The sovereign God, the Creator of all things, has promised to take you through this, and you're going to come out on the other side with a greater sense of intimacy with Him. A greater sense of faith. In other words, because of this adversity, your faith is going to be stronger and your intimacy with God is going to be deeper than ever before.

This is what happens when we keep our focus on Him during the trials—and that's exactly what grace helps us to do. God's grace is sufficient. It's sufficient to release His power, encourage our hearts, remind us of His promises, and recall to us those things that are so essential for you and me to believe and understand.

Another way that grace works to point us to the Father is that it embraces us with the assurance that God is sovereign and is only going to allow so much pain, so much heartache, and so many burdens. He's only going to allow what He knows you and I can bear up under—not in our own strength, but with His strength when we are dependent on Him.

9. "His divine power has given to us all things that pertain to life and godliness, through the knowledge of Him who called us by glory and virtue, by which have been given to us exceedingly great and precious promises, that through these you may be partakers of the divine nature" (2 Peter 1:3–4). What does this passage mean to you personally? What are specific ways God's promises have been proved true in your life?

10. What practical steps will you take this week to intentionally turn your eyes toward your heavenly Father?

Remember that God is sovereign. Allow His grace to embrace you with the assurance there's a limit to adversity. Look to the Father and hear Him say, "You're going to make it. It's going to be okay."

TODAY AND TOMORROW

Today: God's grace is fully available to me in
the moment of my need.

Tomorrow: I will be aware of my desire to quit and I will
choose, with God's help, to keep going.

CLOSING PRAYER

Heavenly Father, we pray today for those who are going through all kinds of adversity. Help us to truly understand the depths of Your grace and know that it is sufficient for whatever problem or crisis that we are facing. Help us to receive by faith that You always have a purpose for the trials we endure—and help us to never quit but to keep on pursuing You in the midst of them. We want to be submissive, willing, and yielded to Your will. We want Your great purpose to be manifest in our lives today. We pray this in Jesus' name and for His sake. Amen.

NOTES AND PRAYER REQUESTS

Use this space to write any key points, questions, or prayer requests from this week's study.

LEADER'S GUIDE

Thank you for choosing to lead your group through this Bible study from Dr. Charles F. Stanley on *Advancing Through Adversity*. The rewards of being a leader are different from those of participating, and it is our prayer that your own walk with Jesus will be deepened by this experience. During the twelve lessons in this study, you will be helping your group members explore key themes related to the topic of trials, challenges, and adversity through teachings by Dr. Charles Stanley and review questions that will encourage group discussion. There are multiple components in this section that can help you structure your lessons and discussion time, so please be sure to read and consider each one.

BEFORE YOU BEGIN

Before your first meeting, make sure your group members each have a copy of *Advancing Through Adversity* so they can follow along in the study guide and have their answers written out ahead of time. Alternately, you can hand out the study guides at your first meeting and give the group members some time to look over the material and ask any preliminary questions. During your first meeting, be sure to send a sheet around the room and have the members write down their name, phone number, and email address so you can keep in touch with them during the week.

To ensure everyone has a chance to participate in the discussion, the ideal size for a group is around eight to ten people. If there are more than ten people, break up the bigger group into smaller subgroups. Make sure the members are committed to participating each week, as this will help create stability and help you better prepare the structure of the meeting.

At the beginning of each meeting, you may wish to start the group time by asking the group members to provide their initial reactions to the material they have read during the week. The goal is to just get the group members' preliminary thoughts—so encourage them at this point to keep their answers brief. Ideally, you want everyone in the group to get a chance to share some of their thoughts, so try to keep the responses to a minute or less.

Give the group members a chance to answer, but tell them to feel free to pass if they wish. With the rest of the study, it's generally not a good idea to have everyone answer every question—a free-flowing discussion is more desirable. But with the opening icebreaker questions, you can go around the circle. Encourage shy people to share, but don't force them. Also, try to keep any one person from dominating the discussion so everyone will have the opportunity to participate.

WEEKLY PREPARATION

As the group leader, there are a few things you can do to prepare for each meeting:

- *Be thoroughly familiar with the material in the lesson.* Make sure you understand the content of each lesson so you know how to structure the group time and are prepared to lead the group discussion.

- *Decide, ahead of time, which questions you want to discuss.* Depending on how much time you have each week, you may not be able to reflect on every question. Select specific questions you feel will evoke the best discussion.

- *Take prayer requests.* At the end of your discussion, be sure to take prayer requests from your group members and then pray for one another.

- *Pray for your group.* Pray for your group members through-out the week and ask that God would lead them as they study His Word.

- *Bring extra supplies to your meeting.* The members should bring their own pens for writing notes, but it's a good idea to have extras available for those who forget. You may also want to bring paper and additional Bibles.

STRUCTURING THE GROUP DISCUSSION TIME

You will need to determine with your group how long you want to meet each week so you can plan your time accordingly. Generally, most groups like to meet for either sixty minutes or ninety minutes, so you could use one of the following schedules:

SECTION	60 Minutes	90 Minutes
WELCOME (group members arrive and get settled)	5 minutes	10 minutes
ICEBREAKER (group members share their initial thoughts regarding the content in the lesson)	10 minutes	15 minutes
DISCUSSION (discuss the Bible study questions you selected ahead of time)	35 minutes	50 minutes
PRAYER/CLOSING (pray together as a group and dismiss)	10 minutes	15 minutes

As the group leader, it is up to you to keep track of the time and keep things moving according to your schedule. If your group is having a good discussion, don't feel the need to stop and move on to the next question. Remember, the purpose is to pull together ideas and share unique insights on the lesson. Encourage everyone to participate, but don't be concerned if certain group members are more quiet. They may just be internally reflecting on the questions and need time to process their ideas before they can share them.

GROUP DYNAMICS

Leading a group study can be a rewarding experience for you and your group members—but that doesn't mean there won't be challenges. Certain members may feel uncomfortable in discussing topics that they consider very personal and might be afraid of being called on. Some members might have disagreements on specific issues. To help prevent these scenarios, consider establishing the following ground rules:

- If someone has a question that may seem off topic, suggest that it is discussed at another time, or ask the group if they are okay with addressing that topic.

- If someone asks a question to which you do not know the answer, confess that you don't know and move on. If you feel comfortable, you can invite the other group members to give their opinions or share their comments based on personal experience.

- If you feel like a couple of people are talking much more than others, direct questions to people who may not have shared yet. You could even ask the more dominating members to help draw out the quiet ones.

- When there is a disagreement, encourage the members to process the matter in love. Invite members from opposing sides to evaluate their opinions and consider the ideas of the other members. Lead the group through Scripture that addresses the topic, and look for common ground.

When issues arise, encourage your group to follow these words from Scripture: "Love one another" (John 13:34), "If it is possible, as much as it depends on you, live peaceably with all men" (Romans 12:18), "Whatever things are true . . . noble . . . pure . . . lovely . . . if there is any virtue and if there is anything praiseworthy—meditate on these things" (Philippians 4:8), and "Be swift to hear, slow to speak, slow to wrath" (James 1:19). This will make your group time more rewarding and beneficial for everyone who attends.

Thank you again for your willingness to lead your group. May God reward your efforts and dedication, equip you to guide your group in the weeks ahead, and make your time together in *Advancing Through Adversity* fruitful for His kingdom.

Also Available in the
Charles F. Stanley Bible Study Series

The Charles F. Stanley Bible Study Series is a unique approach
to Bible study, incorporating biblical truth, personal insights,
emotional responses, and a call to action. Each study draws on
Dr. Stanley's many years of teaching the guiding principles found
in God's Word, showing how we can apply them in practical
ways to every situation we face. This edition of the series has
been completely revised and updated, and includes two
brand-new lessons from Dr. Stanley.

Advancing	Experiencing	Listening	Relying on the
Through Adversity	Forgiveness	to God	Holy Spirit
9780310106555	9780310106579	9780310106593	9780310106616

Available now at your favorite bookstore.
More volumes coming soon.

THOMAS NELSON
Since 1798